T0195939

Praise for *Your Jesus Journey: Navigating Life with Scripture Reflection*

Your Jesus Journey reflects a lifetime of Cindy's personal love for Jesus and her dedication to God's Word. Through years of her investment in our church community, I have witnessed real transformation in the lives of our congregants who followed her simple, clear daily devotions. This book is honest, faithful to the Word, and helpful for personal growth in Christ.

    —Rev. Nathan Alley, pastor of community growth, Christ Community Covenant Church

This book was exactly what I needed! It invited me into deeper dialogue with Jesus as I engaged in the Bible passage. I learned how to capture a summary and apply it to my life. As a result, I've been able to maintain consistent time with the Lord!

    —Heather Wiebel, social worker

The Daily Retreat process has been an excellent way to keep myself firmly rooted in Christ each and every morning. It helps me keep a Christian worldview while conducting my life and has led to me spending more time with Jesus than I ever did before. I wholeheartedly recommend *Your Jesus Journey*, not just as a book but also as a way of developing and deepening your faith.

    —Parker Elliott, Daily Retreat pilot class member

For six years I was blessed to participate in Cindy's Daily Retreat women's group. She wrote her own material, which included a Bible passage, a short example from her life that applied to the reading, questions for us to answer, and applications upon which to meditate. Now she has written this book to fulfill her heart's desire to help all people relate, one-on-one, with Jesus. Enjoy the exciting journey ahead!

    —Patty Davis, Daily Retreat women's group participant

Your Jesus Journey has helped me fill a void in my daily routine—scheduled time alone with Jesus! Cindy's writing is conversational, deep in knowledge, and humorous. She has walked closely with Jesus for many years and, most importantly, has listened to His voice when He gives a command!

    I did Daily Retreat on my own. It's very easy to follow, and the format makes it simple to create a daily habit. I have used both scripture and Christian studies as my base, and it works for both formats.

    —Donni Harms, manuscript proofreader and co-Jesus lover

Your Jesus Journey is an excellent and blessed read. If you are seeking true satisfaction and have not quite found it, this book will be a taste of heaven to you. An intimate relationship with Jesus Christ will carry you through life's fiercest battles. Thank you, Cindy, for being obedient to our Father's call, writing the passions of your heart to encourage others.

    —Marty Harris, retired librarian, Christ Community Covenant Church Council chair, and one of
        Cindy's longtime prayer partners

In one of Cindy's Bible classes, she boldly asked, "At what point does a person cross the line and become completely sold out to Jesus?" This is Cindy to a T. With her amazingly uplifting attitude, she presents Jesus and brings her insights, guidance, and inspirational instruction to the reader on how to have intimacy with Him. I was literally smiling as I read this book because of Cindy's delightful exuberance in spurring on, emboldening, and reassuring the reader that closeness with Jesus is possible. Jesus does not disappoint, and neither will this book. Enjoy the pilgrimage!

    —Lisa Anton, Christ Community Covenant Church

YOUR JESUS JOURNEY

NAVIGATING
LIFE WITH SCRIPTURE
REFLECTION

CINDY OURY

WESTBOW
PRESS®
A DIVISION OF THOMAS NELSON
& ZONDERVAN

WestBow Press books may be ordered through booksellers or by contacting:

WestBow Press
A Division of Thomas Nelson & Zondervan
1663 Liberty Drive
Bloomington, IN 47403
www.westbowpress.com
844-714-3454

Because of the dynamic nature of the Internet, any web addresses or links contained in
this book may have changed since publication and may no longer be valid. The views
expressed in this work are solely those of the author and do not necessarily reflect the views
of the publisher, and the publisher hereby disclaims any responsibility for them.

Any people depicted in stock imagery provided by Getty Images are models,
and such images are being used for illustrative purposes only.
Certain stock imagery © Getty Images.

Scripture quotations marked NIV are taken from the Holy Bible, New
International Version®, NIV®. Copyright © 1973, 1978, 1984 by Biblica, Inc.™
Used by permission of Zondervan. All rights reserved worldwide.

Scripture quotations marked NASB are taken from the New American Standard Bible®, Copyright © 1960,
1962, 1963, 1968, 1971, 1972, 1973, 1975, 1977, 1995 by The Lockman Foundation. Used by permission.

Scripture quotations marked MSG or The Message are taken from The Message. Copyright 1993,
1994, 1995, 1996, 2000, 2001, 2002. Used by permission of NavPress Publishing Group.

Scripture quotations marked NLT are taken from the Holy Bible, New Living Translation,
copyright © 1996, 2004, 2007 by Tyndale House Foundation. Used by permission of
Tyndale House Publishers, Inc., Carol Stream, Illinois 60188. All rights reserved.

ISBN: 979-8-3850-1840-6 (sc)
ISBN: 979-8-3850-1841-3 (e)

Library of Congress Control Number: 2024902346

Print information available on the last page.

WestBow Press rev. date: 02/22/2024

When Jesus was alone with His own disciples, He explained everything.

—Mark 4:34b (NIV)

CONTENTS

PART 1: THE BASICS

PART 2: A NEW APPROACH

PART 3: GAINING MOMENTUM

INTRODUCTION

Hurting? Confused? Feeling distant from God? Not enough time in the day for yourself and your significant others, much less Jesus?

Curious? Interested? Desire refreshment? Need a boost to get out of the recliner of life and onto a pathway of promise?

I get it, and so does Jesus. He's here for you. In fact, He wants to relate to you more than anyone else on the planet right now. He's personal, and He's persistent.

How would I know? For over forty years I've been relating with Him, one-on-one. He has been my answer in times of turmoil, heartache, or exasperation. He's my rock when the rest of life crumbles around me. He's steadfast and immovable when I'm all over the place. He's onto greater plans when I'm still lagging behind. He's all the things I'm not. Over and above all of this, you just can't beat Him for a best friend.

Not long ago, He impressed upon me that it was time to show others how we do this relationship thing since, as unique persons (you) could use encouragement and instruction on exactly how to begin connecting with the Creator. Scripture reflection is a key component to this coalition, which promotes change, insight, usefulness, and adventure in our lives.

Your Jesus Journey is exactly that. Yours—plus Jesus's. No more living vicariously on the voyages of other people. Nope. Jesus desires that you say yes to traveling with Him in tandem throughout this wild pursuit called life. He has bountiful prospects for you. In fact, you are the reason this book was written—because Jesus wants *you* to know Him intimately.

Grab your express ticket for this exciting undertaking with your personal advocate! He's fired up and revving the engine right now.

What are we waiting for? Get in and let's go! Here's to beginning your Jesus journey, with God's Word as your guide.

Your Jesus Journey FAQ

The purpose of this book is to teach everyday people, like you and like me, how to establish and maintain a personal relationship with the Lord Jesus Christ by spending quality time with Him on a regular basis. Here are frequently asked questions (FAQ):

Q: Is this book right for me?

A: Yes, if you

- want to become more intimate with God the Father; Jesus Christ, His Son; and the Holy Spirit.
- struggle to find a way to fit time with the Lord into a busy day.
- want to learn how to read the Bible for personal application.
- want to gain spiritual sight and insight.
- desire a path to peace and fulfillment through the Christian faith.

Q: What will I learn?

A: You will learn how to

- make and take quality time with the Lord on a regular basis.
- read the Bible for deep and heartfelt personal application.
- be humble and teachable before the Lord.
- quickly obey when the Lord reveals a change you should make or an assignment for you to do.
- return to the Lord, day after day, for more of His will for you.

Q: What do I bring?

A: Great question! Please bring

- self-discipline, humility, and a teachable spirit.
- an offering of quality time to give to the Lord each week.
- willingness to practice Daily Retreats (one-on-one time) as the tool for developing a deeper relationship with Jesus Christ.

Q: What is the goal?

A: Spiritual maturity, with

- your spiritual food—the Bible.
- your spiritual workout—daily time with the Lord.
- your spiritual growth—personally applying God's Word and His instructions to your daily life.
- your time frame—a lifelong practice!

Q: What are the rewards of doing this work?

A: Many life-changing rewards, such as,

- an intimate walk with Jesus Christ.
- the fruit of the Spirit: love, joy, peace, patience, kindness, goodness, faithfulness, gentleness, and self-control (Galatians 5:22–23 NIV).
- a new and helpful tool by which to navigate life, whether on bumpy or smooth roads.
- inner peace that passes all understanding.
- clarity about the purpose-filled nature of your life.

HAPPY NEW-APPROACH DAY! KNOWING HIS VOICE ABOVE ALL OTHERS

One of my favorite holidays is New Year's Day. It is a day meant for freshness, when I see before me 365 uncharted days just waiting for unknown treasures to be found and received. If today does not happen to be January 1, then we may call this Happy New-Approach Day to you instead.

I love the spiritual spotlessness that a fork in the road of our spiritual travels brings. It is an opportunity to dedicate new learnings to Jesus and ask Him to grow us up to maturity, keeping us devoted in heart and mind to the purposes He has for us.

In order to follow Jesus on this journey of lifetime, it is imperative that you and I wisely discern His voice above all the other voices that beckon us for attention on a moment-by-moment basis. Jesus explained it perfectly to the Pharisees, a group of snobby, legalistic know-it-alls, who remained in disbelief over the factual miracle that Jesus had restored sight to a blind man. Jesus explained to them that faulty voices (thieves, robbers, and strangers) will vie for their attention, trying to dissuade them from true faith in God. Yet the Good Shepherd can be trusted, and His sheep will know His voice.

> Very truly I tell you Pharisees, anyone who does not enter the sheep pen by the gate, but climbs in by some other way, is a thief and a robber. The one who enters by the gate is the shepherd of the sheep. The gatekeeper opens the gate for him, and the sheep listen to his voice. He calls his own sheep by name and leads them out. When he has brought out all his own, he goes on ahead of them, and his sheep follow him because they know his voice. But they will never follow a stranger; in fact, they will run away from him because they do not recognize a stranger's voice. (John 10:1–5 NIV)

How will you and I know our Good Shepherd's voice? Using verses from the Holy Bible for contemplation assures us of this. We are to "think on the things of God."

> Finally, brothers and sisters, whatever is true, whatever is noble, whatever is right, whatever is pure, whatever is lovely, whatever is admirable—if anything is excellent or praiseworthy—think about such things. (Philippians 4:8 NIV)

Today, on Happy New-Approach Day, there is only one voice I want to follow—the voice of my Lord and Savior, Jesus Christ. I hope this will be a goal of yours as well. Saddle up for the greatest journey you will ever take—the pursuit of intimately knowing His voice above all others and faithfully following it!

How to Use this Book

This book is an instruction manual on intimacy with Jesus Christ. I begin by laying out the primary principles of the Christian faith: who is Jesus, and what is your role in availability and relationship to Him? This foundation is the core of Part 1—"The Basics." The second and third chapters have journal questions for your reflection.

Part 2—"A New Approach" explains how to become more intimate with Jesus Christ. Back in the day, the method I learned and will teach you was most often referred to as "quiet time," a set-aside time with God for reading the Bible and personally reflecting on the meaning of what was just read. As you will discover, Jesus renamed this quiet-time practice that He and I have had for more than forty years. He named it our Daily Retreat time.

After you have learned this new approach to intimacy with Jesus Christ, you'll move on to Part 3—"Gaining Momentum." This section gives a broader, more far-reaching perspective, plus a greater purpose for maintaining this super-connection with Jesus.

Learning Daily Retreat takes practice. You'll receive homework pages, which you may approach in a number of ways:

1. Best-case scenario: When you get to the homework, take five of the next seven to ten days to complete it before moving on in the book. If you were to spend a week on each homework set, you would complete the book in eight to ten weeks. If you have that much time available, then say yes to doing it. Think of it as a class in which you enrolled. Learn along with Jesus, and enjoy a leisurely pace. It will be worth it.

2. If you want to move through more quickly, you can condense the homework and do several days instead of all five. There is great value in each and every day of the homework, but if there's a time crunch, abbreviate. You'll still benefit; even three days a week with Jesus makes a big difference.

3. A third option is to read the book all the way through and then go back to the homework, starting in chapter 2, and do it as prescribed. It will still take you

eight to ten weeks, but you will be able to focus solely on the practice of Daily Retreat when you come back to it.

4. This program is a superb weekly study group tool. Read an assigned chapter each week, do the homework, and meet to discuss. The support and accountability in this arrangement is ideal.

You will notice that throughout our journey together, you will come across several recurring themes, especially the topics of humility and obedience. I urge you to be open to gleaning how these reappearing subjects speak to your life as you move through the Daily Retreat process.

After each homework lesson, beginning in chapter 4, you may fill out a Daily Retreat evaluation form, if desired. These are to aid you in finding the best approach for you. Here are the questions, along with a helpful Bible verse for each. Please refer back to this page if you would like to refer to the scripture reference for a particular question.

1. **What worked for you?**
   The reward of humility and the fear of the Lord are riches, honor, and life. (Proverbs 22:4 NASB)

2. **What did not work for you? What was difficult? What needs to change?**
   I will lead the blind by a way they do not know, in paths they do not now I will guide them. I will make darkness into light before them, and rugged places into plains. These are the things I will do. (Isaiah 42:16 NASB)

3. **Pray over the difficulties together with God.**
   No weapon formed against you will prosper. (Isaiah 54:17a NASB)

4. **What did you learn? How did the Lord speak to you or use you?**
   Call to Me and I will answer you and show you great and mighty things which you do not know. (Jeremiah 33:3 NASB)

   Then I heard the voice of the Lord saying, "Whom shall I send and who will go for Us?" Then I said, "Here am I, Lord. Send me." (Isaiah 6:8 NASB)

5. **What excites you? What are your hopes?**
   Christ is not weak toward you, but mighty in you. (2 Corinthians 13:3 NASB)

Remember, you have a travel coach, Jesus, who goes along with you every step of the way. He will help see you through to the end. After all, this book was His idea in the first place, as He yearns to relate one-on-one with you. Therefore, He most certainly will boost you to success.

If you have difficulties along the way or would like support, you will find some suggestions at my website: YourJesusJourney.net/Contact

Thank you for joining in this great adventure. Find the way that works for you, and go for it!

PART 1

THE BASICS

Trail to Mount Shasta, California

JESUS

The All-Important First Step: Know Personally the One You Are Following

Have you given your life over to Jesus Christ as Lord and Savior? If so, what a blessing! The knowledge that you are no longer in charge of yourself but that Jesus has become your commander in chief allows the very first step of the journey to begin.

If you are searching, curious, or investigating what your Jesus journey is all about, then welcome! Consider this a place where you will be encouragingly supported along the way in your own personal exploration.

Most believers are able to pinpoint a time in the past when the act of giving their hearts to Jesus, once and for all, took place. For me, it was in February 1982. My husband of eight months led me to the Lord—although it had been a process that was three years in the making. I remember saying, "I've had a system of belief for twenty-two years and am unable to change that on my own. I'm not even going to try. If God is real, He will have to change my heart for me instead."

Well, that was just the invitation Jesus was looking for. He started in then and continues to refine my heart to this very day.

If you cannot recall making a specific decision for Jesus Christ, or if it has been a process of new revelations that have brought you down this interesting path of a brand-new relationship with Him, then please consider making this day, today, the day you say yes to the gift of salvation God has for you. The prayer below, when prayed from the heart, will open the doors of forgiveness, eternity, and abundant life here on earth to you.

Dear God, I am a sinner in need of forgiveness and grace. It is astonishing to me that You know everything about me and still love me. I believe that Jesus Christ, Your Son, took the punishment I deserve, due to the sin that so easily entangles me, and laid down His perfect life for me on the cross. Three days later, He rose up from the grave to conquer sin and death forevermore. Christ's blood and sacrifice have made me clean and completely forgiven. I will follow You now, Jesus, step by step, as You transform me and show me Your will for my life. There is nowhere else I would rather be and no one else I would rather follow. Amen.

If this was your heartfelt prayer, congratulations on making the most important decision of any person's lifetime. Jesus is by your side right now. This is the moment He's been waiting for all of your life—to redeem you.

Goodbye, Darkness; the Light of Life Is Here

Once you and I accept Jesus's lordship in our lives, He begins to dispel spiritual darkness or our own ignorance of heavenly things and opens our eyes to His divine light instead. A few years ago, a blurb in our church bulletin tugged at my heart. It was a child's testimony of how her week at church camp had influenced her life. Annie said, "God opened my eyes all the way to the light. Before, I was just squinting." How precious! How observant!

I am in full agreement with her, as was the man born blind at birth, whom Jesus healed on the Sabbath in order to show the glory of God to the unbelieving Pharisees. The Pharisees were an elite group of judiciaries who followed and monitored every jot and tittle of the Jewish law to an unreasonable fault.

> They brought to the Pharisees the man who had been blind. Now the day on which Jesus had made the mud and opened the man's eyes was a Sabbath.[1] Therefore the Pharisees also asked him how he had received his sight. "He put mud on my eyes," the man replied, "and I washed, and now I see." Some of the Pharisees said, "This man is not from God, for he does not keep the Sabbath." But others asked, "How can a sinner perform such signs?" So they were divided ... Jesus said, "For judgment

---

[1] The Sabbath was the day when Jews were not to do any work. Since the healing was done on this day, the Pharisees concluded Jesus was a sinner. The question came down to, "Is healing work, or is it a gift?"

I have come into this world, so that the blind will see[2] and those who see will become blind."[3] (John 9:13–16, 39 NIV)

This is the story of every one of us who has had Jesus Christ dispel our darkness of sin, shame, and guilt and show us His light of forgiveness, acceptance, and truth instead. Jesus says,

I am the light of the world. Whoever follows me will never walk in darkness, but will have the light of life. (John 8:12 NIV)

May you and I allow our squinting eyes to open widely, as Annie, the precious young believer, did at church camp. Let us look inwardly and upwardly and walk onward into the light of our Lord and Savior, Jesus Christ.

JESUS CALLS YOU FRIEND

In Luke 5, Jesus begins His ministry with His friends. Some of these people never expected that Jesus would take particular interest in them, while others sought Him because they had problems they couldn't handle on their own.

What about you? Have you been looking for Jesus, or has He found you? On our journeys through life, Jesus wants not only to steer our vehicles but also, as our friend, to ride "shotgun" with us wherever we go.

1. Jesus befriends everyday people. You and I are everyday people. We live decent lives, provide for our families, teach our children right from wrong, enjoy our time off, and live by a set of decent moral standards. We have our share of struggles and bounce back by putting one foot in front of the other once again.

After Jesus had finished teaching a large crowd of people on the banks of the Sea of Galilee, He took special notice of Simon (soon to be known as Peter), Andrew, James, and John, local fishermen who had been listening in dejectedly after a long night of coming up empty.

When He had finished speaking, He said to Simon, "Put out into deep water, and let down the nets for a catch." Simon answered, "Master, we've worked hard all night and haven't caught anything. But because you say so, I will let down the nets." When they had done so, they

---

[2] Jesus taught that true spiritual sight brings about a change of heart.

[3] Likewise, those who claim to see just fine without Jesus will be blinded to spiritual sight.

caught such a large number of fish that their nets began to break …
Then Jesus said to Simon, "Don't be afraid; from now on you will fish
for people." So they pulled their boats up on shore, left everything and
followed Him. (Luke 5:4–6, 10b–11 NIV)

Jesus befriended these four everyday people, inviting them to go along with Him on the ride of their lives. He does the same for us. He knows what we've been up against and is ready to replace our emptiness with His fullness. By the way, Jesus's prophecy proved true. You and I are two of the people in their nets!

2. Jesus befriends outcasts. Some of Jesus's friends seek Him because there is absolutely nowhere else to turn. These beloveds are not disappointed with their return on investment.

While Jesus was in one of the towns, a man came along who was
covered with leprosy. When he saw Jesus, he fell with his face to the
ground and begged Him, "Lord, if you are willing, you can make
me clean." Jesus reached out His hand and touched the man. "I am
willing," he said. "Be clean!" And immediately the leprosy left him.
(Luke 5:12–13 NIV)

Friend, you are no longer an outcast in the eyes of Jesus. He is willing, and He will cleanse the hurt from within your heart, giving you testimony as to what He has done for you as well.

3. Jesus befriends the ill, and Jesus also befriends the faithful. Oftentimes, illness and faithfulness are paired. In illness, we are at the bottom of ourselves, needing aid and treatment from an outside source. Faithfulness rallies from friends and family who offer themselves as fellow travelers in this large passenger van of support.

One day Jesus was teaching, and Pharisees and teachers of the law were
sitting there. They had come from every village of Galilee and from
Judea and Jerusalem. And the power of the Lord was with Jesus to heal
the sick. Some men came carrying a paralyzed man on a mat and tried
to take him into the house to lay him before Jesus. When they could
not find a way to do this because of the crowd, they went up on the
roof and lowered him on his mat through the tiles into the middle of
the crowd, right in front of Jesus.

When Jesus saw their faith, he said, "Friend, your sins are forgiven."

The Pharisees and the teachers of the law began thinking to themselves, "Who is this fellow who speaks blasphemy? Who can forgive sins but God alone?"

Jesus knew what they were thinking and asked, "Why are you thinking these things in your hearts? Which is easier: to say, 'Your sins are forgiven,' or to say, 'Get up and walk'? But I want you to know that the Son of Man has authority on earth to forgive sins." So, He said to the paralyzed man, "I tell you, get up, take your mat and go home." And immediately, as everyone watched, the man jumped up, picked up his mat, and went home praising God. (Luke 5:17–25 NIV)

Faithful friend, you will never be disappointed in Jesus. He will prove faithful to you. Friend who is ill, you will receive healing, either here or in heaven. Jesus hears your prayers and is with you, moment by moment. Allow Him to minister to you, along with your faithful friends, family, and caregivers.

4. Jesus befriends people who long for a second chance. Perhaps, along the backroads of the wilderness, you became lost. You went along various paths, trying to find your way to fulfillment. None of the trails you wandered led to what you'd envisioned, and now you're clambering up a steep precipice, directionless. Hang on! Guide Jesus heads your way, as His specialty is finding the lost. He leaves the group of ninety-nine behind for a moment to find the one and only you!

After this, Jesus went out and saw a tax collector [considered by the Jews as scum and traitorous] by the name of Levi sitting at his tax booth. "Follow Me," Jesus said to him, and Levi got up, left everything and followed Him … But the Pharisees and the teachers of the law who belonged to their sect complained to His disciples, "Why do you eat and drink with tax collectors and sinners?" Jesus answered them, "It is not the healthy who need a doctor, but the sick. I have not come to call the righteous, but sinners to repentance." (Luke 5:27–28, 30–32 NIV)

Friend, Jesus holds the map of your life in His capable hands. Leaving the past behind, He holds the key to your brand-new future, with an individualized route for you all planned.

Which of the five friend types describes you? Do you consider yourself befriended by Jesus? You'd better believe it! Jesus most certainly calls you *friend* and has staked His life on you.

> Greater love has no one than this: to lay down one's life for one's friends. (John 15:1 3 NIV)

SALVATION IN A NUTSHELL: JOHN 3:16

Salvation in Jesus Christ is not difficult. It is easily available to any and all who want it. The most well-known verse of scripture, John 3:16, explains succinctly the purpose of the entire Bible and of God's desired relationship with each of us:

> For God so loved the world that He gave His one and only Son, that whoever believes in Him shall not perish but have eternal life. (NIV)

Plain and simple. Believe in Jesus Christ, God's Son, and in His sacrificial death and Resurrection for sinners like you and like me. Then, receive the greatest gift of all, eternal life. It can't get much more effortless than that. Yet issues like pride, self-sufficiency, and the distractions of the world get in the way, complicating the concept's straightforwardness.

With singleness of purpose, however, there is life-altering force in those words. For two thousand-plus years, John 3:16 has brought countless individuals to faith since Jesus's Resurrection. We should not let anything complicate its power to move us from the sentence of death and loss to winning everlasting life with Jesus Christ.

Hear clearly the cheers for your own victory, not only from me but also from all the saints in glory who traveled their own personal Jesus journeys and received the prize!

TIME FOR REFLECTION

It is helpful to take periodic breaks to mull over the reading thus far and your reaction to it. On the following page, please take fifteen to twenty minutes (or more, if necessary) to write down your answers to the seven questions.

REST STOP: QUESTIONS TO PONDER

Date:

1. Regarding the introduction, what rings true for you?

2. Regarding the FAQ, what do you need most in your life at this moment?

3. Regarding "Happy New-Approach Day," why is a new approach reason to celebrate? Which voices have guided you in the past? Why might Jesus's voice be different from the world's voices?

4. Regarding "The All-Important First Step," what brought you to this point right now in your life? Have you made a decision to follow Jesus Christ? Could you commit to reading this book all the way through to find out many reasons to do so?

5. Regarding "Goodbye Darkness," why do you need spiritual sight? What makes spiritual sight different from regular sight?

6. Regarding "Jesus Calls You Friend," which type of friend best describes you: an everyday person, an outcast, a person who is ill or infirm, a faithful person, a person who has made wrong choices and needs a second chance? (More than one may fit for you.)

7. Regarding "Salvation in a Nutshell," why do people complicate the simple message of salvation? Is it easy or difficult for you to believe in Jesus as your Savior?

Vedauwoo Trail near Laramie, Wyoming

2

YOU AND ME

THE SECOND HALF OF A DYNAMIC DUO

After learning about Jesus and His role in our lives as Savior, guide, and friend, let's now look at the second half of this dynamic duo—you and me. As Jesus seeks to partner with us, He asks us to take several questions under thoughtful consideration:

- Do you want to get well?
- Do you believe I have authority to forgive your sins once and for all?
- Do I have your permission to change your heart?
- May I be your boss?
- Will you receive My wise counsel?
- Will you make time for Me because the time is near?
- Will you see yourself as I see you?

Hmmm. Tough questions. Let's examine them one by one.

DO YOU WANT TO GET WELL?

"Do you want to get well?" This question was posed by Jesus to a paralytic man who had been an invalid for thirty-eight years. What would your answer or mine be? How about "Of course!" Instead, this man responded with his completely understandable reason for why he could not get better on his own:

"Sir," the invalid replied, "I have no one to help me into the pool when the water is stirred. While I am trying to get in, someone else goes down ahead of me." (John 5:7 NIV)

As with every query Jesus makes, He would like you and me to turn His question inward, applying it spiritually to our inner lives. "Cindy, do you want to get well spiritually?"

"_____ [insert your name here], do you want to get well spiritually?"

Do you or I always respond, "Of course!"?

There are many seemingly valid justifications why you or I refuse to go to the next level with Jesus.

- I've never believed in God or Jesus. I don't even think they are real.
- I've been deeply hurt, physically, emotionally, or spiritually, by others.
- I was raised this way to believe these things about myself and others. I can't change that.
- The person who wronged me has never asked for my forgiveness, so why should I forgive that person when the injustice was done to me?
- I don't know what the outcome will be if I place my faith in Christ for this request. What if the answer isn't what I want?
- This is just the way I am. I've always been irritable, angry, fearful, nagging, discontented, outspoken, pessimistic, sarcastic, selfish, haughty, uncertain, unable, a failure, and so on. How can I change now?
- I can't get well in my own strength. I've tried. It's easier to live with my spiritual malady. This must be my lot in life.

Yet Jesus places a life-changing choice before us and asks us to make strides for the better. He urges, "Say goodbye to what paralyzes you, and allow Me the pleasure of bringing greater spiritual health and peace to your life. Pick yourself up from frustration and walk with Me to spiritual victory."

I've experienced spiritual healing in every one of these categories. Today, I've named yet another spiritual malady in which I've tried in my own strength to master yet have failed. You and I are spiritual works in progress, gaining footing and eventually freedom with every spiritual infirmity we give to Him.

May you and I find greater spiritual freedom by picking up our mats, which once held the immobilized, and bravely move forward with Jesus.

DO YOU BELIEVE I HAVE AUTHORITY TO FORGIVE YOUR SINS ONCE AND FOR ALL?

While I received the gift of salvation in February 1982, I did not accept the spiritual health that was due me until February 2000. Although I should have received both, I was shackled in the prison of inner guilt, unwilling to forgive myself for a wrong and unworthy past. It wasn't that I was unfruitful during those first eighteen years after I said yes to Jesus's lordship of my life. Conversely, I consumed Bible studies and relished in Jesus's revealing of Himself to me. I learned how to walk with Him and grew tremendously during that era.

Jesus, however, knew more about me than I knew about myself. He knew that in an inner crypt of my heart, there remained two festering issues: personal guilt and unconfessed sin to someone with whom I had been untruthful, my husband. Because Jesus knew me so well and loved me so deeply, He wanted me to deal with this hindrance in my spiritual life. I, too, knew that I could not proceed forward with Him if this issue remained much longer, for out of the crypt it had crept. The poisonous, hidden wound had been punctured at long last and was seeping into my system.

While I longed to confess to my husband how I had wronged him, I was completely terrified to do so. Every time the Lord would say, "Now is the time," I would cower away. I began to see my kind, loving Savior as a harsh taskmaster, shouting the words, "Do it now!" while bringing the whip down painfully across my back, instead of hearing those words as He truly said them—with wise, gentle urging.

Finally, when I could no longer endure the pain of the lashing whip, I took my husband on a getaway, knowing full well that the result of this private escape could be devastating to us. Yet I also realized that I must be obedient to my assignment, regardless of the result.

I sat my husband down, confessing what had been festering for eighteen years. When I had concluded my admission, with eyes closed and body tense, ready to receive another lash of the whip, I heard my husband utter just one word—a reply that would change my life forever.

"So?"

So? So? *So?* I was stupefied. Why had I imprisoned myself for eighteen years with guilt, shame, and hidden heartache when the answer could have been, "So what?" so long ago? At that moment, I had a vision of the heavy ball and chain of my disgrace, which had hung weightily around my neck, being lifted away in the delicate beaks of two doves and taken up into the heavens, never to be seen or felt again.

I was lighter than air. My perception of my sweet Savior changed immediately.

No longer a harsh taskmaster, Jesus was now my loving redeemer, who sought and insisted upon my full freedom—a liberty that I had refused until that very moment. Jesus, in His compassion for me, a repentant sinner, had used my faithful, forgiving husband to be His voice of final reconciliation.

Just as Jesus spoke with tenderness to the paralytic man, so He spoke to me that day. "Cindy, your sins are forgiven. Rise up from the pit of damnation and come forward with Me to a new and abundant life." And, as it says in Luke 5:25, "at once [s] he rose up before them, and went home glorifying God" (NIV).

If you, like the paralytic or like me, need spiritual health and liberation once and for all, I urge you to meet with Jesus and/or someone you trust to confess the sin that has you incapacitated and claim the freedom that has already been granted to you, once and for all, by the authority of Jesus Christ Himself. Amen, dear friend, amen. "Your sins are forgiven!" (Luke 5:20 NIV).

Do I Have Your Permission to Change Your Heart?

As you and I study the life of Jesus, one thing becomes extremely clear: Jesus cares only about our hearts and the actions that result from their contents. Is your heart hard or soft, closed or open, unwilling or agreeable, dead or pulsing? It is interesting that a person can be fully alive, yet if a hardened heart resides in the inner person, Jesus regards him or her as a concealed tomb. Likewise, He will spare no expense to reveal Himself to the one whose heart is soft, pliable, teachable, and obedient.

To have a relationship with Jesus is to have the Great Physician perform open-heart surgery on us, ridding us of impurities and stubborn blockages, filling our hearts instead with spiritual truths that have significance unto eternity. Let us willingly decide to book our calendars with divine appointments with our extraordinary heart surgeon!

Additionally, Father God desired this same inner purity of heart for His chosen people, the Jewish nation of Israel. While reading the book of Deuteronomy, I stumbled upon this very interesting set of verses concerning desert housekeeping for the wandering Israelites:

> Designate a place outside the camp where you can go to relieve yourself. As part of your equipment have something to dig with, and when you relieve yourself, dig a hole and cover up your excrement. For the Lord your God moves about in your camp to protect you and to deliver your enemies to you. Your camp must be holy, so that he

will not see among you anything indecent and turn away from you. (Deuteronomy 23:12–14 NIV)

In applying this scripture spiritually, the Lord God desires that our camps—His inner dwelling place in the depths of our beings—be holy.

As I have shared, when I first began this new, intimate relationship with Jesus, I had a ton of waste in my heart, and Jesus and I began quick work of unloading my life of it. Jesus assured me that what I had carried inside my body for years was merely useless baggage—refuse and nothing more. He compelled me to bury the dung of my past sins and poor choices far away from His new abode, which He tidied daily.

Good riddance, old me! Welcome, Jesus, housekeeper extraordinaire, who has turned my now–squeaky-clean heart into His permanent home. Let Him do the very same for you right now.

MAY I BE YOUR BOSS?

What characteristics envelop the perfect boss? Would you agree with these qualities? Authority with appreciation. Comprehension with compassion. Knowledge with kindness. Power with passion. In the parables of Jesus, certain characters display the attributes of God, and certain ones display the human idiosyncrasies common to each of us.

In Jesus's most classic parable of all, the Prodigal Son (see Luke 15:11–32), the father is symbolic of our gracious heavenly Father, who has all the attributes of the above great boss—one whom you and I should not mind following.

The prodigal son depicts our self-centeredness in not wanting to trust the authority who has our best interests at heart. In the story, the youngest son of a wealthy father requested his inheritance early. He was given it graciously by his father, ran away to "Vegas," squandered all his newly received wealth on wild living, and then, poverty-stricken, was forced to take a menial job, feeding the disgusting, defiling pigs in a pigsty. The turning point of the parable comes when the son realizes his long string of mistakes. A simple phrase describes the moment: "When he came to his senses" (Luke 15:17 NIV).

I remember this same came-to-his-senses moment as depicted in an old television commercial. A man smacks himself on the forehead with the palm of his hand and says, "Wow! I could have chosen delicious vegetable juice instead!" His realization was that of all the drink options out there, only one provided the most nutrition with the added benefit of good taste and, as is always the case, had been promoted by a higher authority. Alas, after choosing sugary soda instead, the man's cognition changed. He came to his senses, perceiving that the better choice would have been to follow the sage advice of someone above him.

How often have you and I been in a mess, jam, bad habit, or failure? We may stay in that awful place indefinitely, or we, too, can come to our senses with a change in behavior. We can take a new direction, accept wise counsel, and pray for God's redemptive grace to miraculously take over our situations. This act of coming to our senses is the first step toward new life—a life in submission to a great boss.

The prodigal returned home, was accepted back into the father's open arms, and was finally welcomed, with banquet and ring, back into the fold. Like the prodigal before us, relinquishing our own agendas for the better agenda of an all-knowing boss and omniscient heavenly Father brings rescue and relief to us as well.

WILL YOU RECEIVE WISE COUNSEL FROM ME?

What stress, anxiety, or trouble fills your life today? What looms overhead, causing thoughts of, *How am I ever to manage this?* Right now, fill in the following blanks with your top three personal concerns:

1._____

2._____

3. _____

In Matthew 6:25–26, Jesus impressed upon me that I am not to stress out about any of my above concerns because He loves me personally and takes pleasure in caring for me today. As you read Jesus's encouragement to you, insert your name in the brackets. Place parentheses around the phrases that are stresses. Underline the phrases that show Christ's compassion and care for your personal needs.

> Therefore I tell you [_____], do not worry about your life, what you will eat or drink; or about your body, what you will wear. Is not life more than food, and the body more than clothes? Look at the birds of the air; they do not sow or reap or store away in barns, and yet your heavenly Father feeds them. Are you [_____] not much more valuable than they? (Matthew 6:25–26 NIV)

This wise counsel is ours for the taking. Let us, then, rest in His care, because He's got us covered. Spend time with Jesus, our wonderful counselor, as He longs to minister to us where we hurt the most. Destressing our days is what Jesus's wise counsel is all about. A few moments a day with Him brings health to the soul.

WILL YOU MAKE TIME FOR ME BECAUSE THE TIME IS NEAR?

Time! It is a precious commodity that takes continual monitoring. For most of us, there isn't enough of it. "If only there were more hours in a day!" we cry out. Two facts are certain regarding time: (1) time is fleeting, and (2) one day, our time on this earth will be finished. The new question becomes, "How do I make the most of my time?"

One call of scripture, which speaks to the fleeting aspect of time, is to spend a portion of our precious twenty-four hours with God as an investment, from which we receive a great benefit. Hosea 10:12 is a beautiful picture of this:

> Sow righteousness for yourselves, reap the fruit of unfailing love, and break up your unplowed ground; for it is time to seek the Lord until he comes and showers his righteousness on you. (NIV)

Revelation 1:3 addresses the finality of time and our blessings because we have understood time's urgency in advance:

> Blessed is the one who reads aloud the words of this prophecy [or scripture/Holy Bible], and blessed are those who hear it and take to heart what is written in it, because the time is near. (NIV)

One of the most reflective choices we can make is to go to God and ask Him to reveal His will for us regarding our time. My prayer for each of us is that when all is said and done, God will be pleased with how we apportion our time each day. Today, enjoy the healthful benefits of taking time with Him concerning the time you will set aside for Him.

WILL YOU SEE YOURSELF AS I SEE YOU?

Have you ever read the Old Testament book Song of Solomon, written by King Solomon, son of King David? It is a very personal, sensual story of two lovers and their desire for each other. My goodness, these two have got it going on—a power couple much like Romeo and Juliet. Spring has sprung, and love is in the air!

What sort of questions to ponder do the verses in this book bring about? Women, would you say your lips were "like a scarlet ribbon"? Men, how close are your legs to being "pillars of marble set on bases of pure gold"? Hmmm. It seems as if spiritual lessons are lacking in the book of Song of Solomon.

But as I read it anew, one verse popped out at me. I couldn't stop thinking about it:

> You are altogether beautiful, my darling; there is no flaw in you. (Song of Solomon 4:7 NIV)

Isn't this the way we start out in dating, engagement, and early marriage, thinking our partners are totally flawless? Then reality sets in. Wait a minute—he leaves the toilet seat up. Hold on a second—she doesn't cook like Mom. Suddenly, we realize we are relating with someone who has many flaws. On occasion, romance, respect, and love have diminishing returns because of that reality.

The quality of flawlessness begins and ends with our Triune God: Father, Son, and Holy Spirit. Flawlessness is personified in Jesus Christ. Then, as mind-boggling as this may seem, it is transferred to you and to me by our acceptance of Jesus Christ's sacrificial death on the cross as a covering for our sins and multitudinous flaws. In the eyes of Father God, if we have accepted His free gift of salvation through His Son's sacrificial death and Resurrection in our places, we are now deemed flawless. Jesus says to you and to me,

> [Your name here,] you are altogether beautiful … there is no flaw in you." (Song of Solomon 4:7 NIV)

Who, me? You've got to be kidding, right? Nope. He's not kidding. God has imputed Christ's righteousness onto us—the perfect life of Jesus cashed in for a messed-up one like mine. This is a truth and concept that must sink in very deeply in order to be fathomed. The apostle Paul, writing to the believers in Corinth, penned these words about this transfer of righteousness:

> God made Christ who had no sin to be sin for us, so that in Him we might become the righteousness of God. (2 Corinthians 5:21 NIV)

Incredible! If you and I receive this new distinction of being flawless in His sight, shouldn't we see each other as flawless too, despite the physical reality? Are we able, with the Lord's help, to cover another person's flaws and see a new creation in Christ instead? When we see with His eyes, it will be so.

I'm praising God that you and I have been transposed from being full of faults to flawless through the sacrificial love of Jesus Christ.

REST STOP: HOMEWORK TIME

As you and I prepare to keep regular company with Jesus Christ, it is a stellar idea to take a look deep inside the inner recesses of our souls to see if we are open to His entry into our lives in such a personal way. Thus, the homework for chapter 2 is all about examining our own lives for receptivity, which is a willingness to accept a new idea and make a needed change.

You most effectively will complete the following five homework pages in five consecutive days, one day at a time, taking about twenty to thirty minutes to ponder and reflect per day.

I know, I know. You don't necessarily want to pull off at this rest stop. Let's keep moving instead! Let's progress!

I promise that you will progress rapidly on the road to relationship with Jesus but let us allow Him to set the pace. You will experience Jesus each day of the next five, as you contemplate with Him the answers to His questions.

Warning! Just as my own crypt of compacted crud was buried below the surface, you, too, may find that your decayed dregs of the past are unearthed in this process. The object is to deal with them with Jesus, remove them from your life, and move on as a flawless being, ready to fill all the newly open spaces in your swept-out soul with the love and affirmations of Jesus.

If, by chance, you decide to read the entire book from cover to cover without doing the homework, then I hope you will return to this page (go ahead; turn down the page corner now) and restart from here, the second time through, for real. Jesus is counting on you to establish what He desires—the alliance of your heart with His.

Thank you for taking the next five days to contemplate with Jesus your readiness for this major merger. He is primed and passionate to show Himself to you in these next days.

PERSONAL INVENTORY HOMEWORK DAY 1: HEART SURGERY

Date:

1. How willing am I to examine my own heart for things that may hinder me from spiritual forward progress? How will this be possible?

2. Reflecting on "Do You Want to Get Well?": In which areas do I need spiritual healing?

3. How willing am I to allow Jesus to heal me of these maladies? If so, what must I surrender to Him right now?

4. How easy is it for me to say I'm sorry to others? How easy is it for me to say I'm sorry to God? Why is saying I'm sorry necessary?

5. Reflecting on "Do You Believe I Have Authority to Forgive Your Sins Once and for All?": Do I believe that my sins have been forgiven once and for all? Why or why not? What evidence of this belief is seen in my life, or how may I begin to live this out?

6. Reflecting on "Do I Have Permission to Change Your Heart?": How willing am I to change for the better, based on the Lord's desires for my life? How do I respond when confronted by another regarding my own negative behavior? How will I respond when Jesus shows me an area in my life that displeases Him?

PERSONAL INVENTORY HOMEWORK DAY 2: WHO'S THE BOSS?

Date:

1. How do I define the following words?

   Prideful
   Entitled
   Humble
   Submissive

2. How do I "measure up" to my own standards? How do I measure up to God's standards? Who has made it possible for me to ever measure up?

3. Have I asked Jesus Christ to be my personal Savior? If so, when? If not, why might I consider doing so?

4. Reflecting on Jesus's question, "May I Be Your Boss?": Who is the current boss of my life? Why does Jesus want to apply for this job? What value is there in Jesus becoming the boss of my life?

5. How will I respond when my boss tells me to do something I do not want to do? How does John 14:23–24 sit with me?

   Jesus replied, "Anyone who loves me will obey my teaching. My Father will love them, and we will come to them and make our home with them. Anyone who does not love me will not obey my teaching. These words you hear are not my own; they belong to the Father who sent me." (NIV)

PERSONAL INVENTORY HOMEWORK
DAY 3: RECEIVING WISE COUNSEL

Date:

1. Reflecting on "Will You Receive My Wise Counsel?": Who wants me to be a better person? Why? How does the following verse apply? (*Sanctified* means taking on the characteristics of Jesus.)

   It is God's will that you should be sanctified. (1 Thessalonians 4:3a NIV)

2. How do I define the following words?

   Advice
   Counsel

3. Whose advice do I trust? Why? How does Proverbs 19:20 apply?

   Listen to advice and accept discipline, and at the end you will be counted among the wise. (NIV)

4. Why is receiving the Lord's counsel to repair inner damage or hurt in my life a worthwhile endeavor?

5. To what lengths will I go to implement His counsel in all areas of my life?

6. Will I forgive? If so, who needs my forgiveness? When might I offer this forgiveness?

PERSONAL INVENTORY HOMEWORK DAY 4:
ALL THE TIME IN THE WORLD

Date:

1. Reflecting on the question "Will You Make Time for Me Because the Time Is Near?": Why is time of the essence in learning from Jesus?

2. To make room in my day for one-on-one time with Jesus, let me consider my weekly routine. Where are my thirty-minute open slots of time, from the moment I arise to the time I go to bed? Are these open times conducive to quiet reflection time?

3. What might I eliminate or rearrange to make some open reflection time? How might trading one of my activities for one-on-one time with Jesus be a possibility?

4. Where might I fit in three to five consistent twenty- to thirty-minute slots of time?

5. Jesus's time with His Father was before His day started. Why?

   Very early in the morning, while it was still dark, Jesus got up, left the house and went off to a solitary place, where he prayed. (Mark 1:35 NIV)

6. Shall I start my days earlier so as to be taught by Jesus?

   But when Jesus was alone with His own disciples, He explained everything. (Mark 4:34b NIV)

PERSONAL INVENTORY HOMEWORK DAY 5:
SEEING MYSELF THROUGH JESUS'S EYES

Date:

1. Reflecting on the question "Will You See Yourself as I [Jesus] See You?": Here is a list of mind-boggling concepts regarding my salvation. (For example, Jesus loves me just the way I am.)

2. Who fits the definition of true flawlessness?

   He is the Rock, his works are perfect, and all his ways are just. A faithful God who does no wrong, upright and just is he. (Deuteronomy 32:4 NIV)

3. Once I accept God's gift of salvation through the death and Resurrection of Jesus, who took the punishment I deserved upon Himself, how does God then see me?

   But now, this is what the Lord says—he who created you, Jacob, he who formed you, Israel: "Do not fear, for I have redeemed you; I have summoned you by name; you are mine." (Isaiah 43:1 NIV)

4. Because I have been forgiven once and for all and now am deemed "flawless" in the eyes of Jesus, how does that lift me up to a greater vision for myself?

5. What hopes and dreams might I now be able to accomplish with Christ's help?

COMPANY IS COMING!

Congratulations on completing the personal inventory homework. Perhaps you had some tough days, searching your heart. Perhaps you felt relieved that, with Jesus, the future is bright with hope and promise because, after all, we are forgiven and redeemed.

Guess what? Company is coming! How do you and I usually get ready for a house guest? We clean up. Imagine an out-of-towner using an unclean shower, toilet, or towel. Yuck! For special travelers, you and I most certainly take the time necessary to spray, scrub, and scour the inside of the tub and toilet as well as the outside.

Prior to the beginning of Jesus's earthly ministry, John the Baptist's personal assignment was getting the Jews cleaned up and ready for the appearance of Jesus, the most unrivaled visitor of all. Sin and soot needed to be washed away from the inside of the heart in preparation for their majestic Messiah's coming (see Mark 1:1–4).

So, too, our hearts have been adequately prepared for the arrival of King Jesus, the most glorious guest we shall ever host and truly heavenly company. Let us open the doors of our hearts to our kingly caller in order that we might entertain the thoughts of our worthy Prince of Peace.

TRAIL AT CRATER LAKE NATIONAL PARK, OREGON

3

THE PRACTICE: DAILY RETREAT

RETREAT TO ADVANCE!

What in the world is Daily Retreat? Daily Retreat is the practice of secluding oneself with the Trinity—Father God; His Son, Jesus Christ; and the Holy Spirit—on a regular basis to be guided and directed toward inner and outer change in our personal lives via the method of scripture reflection.

Some years ago, when this book was in its formative stages, I shared its concept with a friend who was also a very strong woman of God. I had only just spoken the words "Daily Retreat" when she interrupted me to exclaim, "I don't want to retreat. I want to advance!" I chuckle now at her Holy Spirit–led comment, knowing that she was partially correct and that I would certainly use her statement and its intended meaning in my book someday.

The goal for a born-again believer in the Lord Jesus Christ is to become more and more like Jesus, not by striving on our own but by allowing the Holy Spirit to transform us into His image. Then, when filled up with God's Word and His truth via the Daily Retreat process, we pour out His love to others in order to advance the kingdom of God—my emboldened friend's part of the equation!

In order to become like Jesus, then, we must know who He is. How better to get to know Jesus than to spend time in His Word, the Holy Bible, studying His traits and His mindset. We also get to know Father God this way, along with His plan of salvation for humankind, which begins in Genesis and ends with Revelation. We become miners, extracting the precious Word of God into our own veins, as opposed to the human-devised philosophies of this world, thus filling our minds with God's way, truth, and life.

Back in the day, this practice was called (and still is by most) "having a quiet time." Jesus, however, proposed a new name that He and I would call this process of spending time with Him. He called it Daily Retreat. As you and I retreat alone with Him each morning, He preps us for the day ahead so that we might advance the kingdom of God to those in our spheres of influence—our own selves, our family members, neighbors, friends, coworkers, and community members.

Jeremiah 15:19 says that when you and I mine for gold nuggets in the Word of God by going into the inner recesses of the heart, then, when we come out into the real world, we become transformed into leaders who influence others for Christ.

> Therefore, thus says the Lord, "If you return, then I will restore you— Before Me you will stand; And if you extract the precious from the worthless, you will become My spokesperson. They [your sphere of influence] for their part may turn to you, but as for you, you must not turn to them. (Jeremiah 15:19 NASB)

My Daily Retreat Testimony

For more than forty years, I have been a follower of Jesus Christ. In that time, I have been involved in many Bible studies, small groups, church activities, and other informative classes that have helped in my spiritual growth. Yet nothing has meant so much to me as getting to know Jesus Christ personally through my own daily devotional time.

Thirty years ago, I began asking the Lord Himself to be my teacher—just the two of us. I gave Him my best time, early in the morning, and my undivided attention. With the help of my Bible and a journal, I asked Jesus to reveal Himself to me and to let me be like Mary, who chose to sit at His feet and learn, rather than to be like Martha, who was worried and bothered much of the time (see Luke 10:38–42). My love for Jesus Christ and His love for me bloomed.

Twenty or so years ago, an acquaintance asked me to go along with a group of women for a spiritual get-away weekend. It had been several years since I had attended one, but because of my home situation—I had six preschool, elementary, and teenaged children who each had various activities requiring my assistance and attention, a husband who traveled five days of the week, and a mother I helped several times a week—I did not feel that I could go. More importantly, I did not feel led by the Holy Spirit to go.

The woman said, "With all you do and your busy life as it is, I would be running out the door as fast as possible. Don't you just want to get away from everything, even for a weekend?"

The next morning, as I was spending time with the Lord, I poured my heart out to Him and said, "Jesus, why don't I feel the need to go? Is there something wrong with me?"

His reply to me was this: *"The reason you do not feel led to go on this retreat is that you have a Daily Retreat with Me. Each day, we spend quality time together, and the blessing you receive for sitting at My feet on a regular basis is a peace that passes all understanding and a calm spirit in the midst of the daily trials of life."*

There was my answer. I had a Daily Retreat with my Lord and Savior, Jesus Christ. My time with Him was rich and renewing as I read the Bible and reflected on how His Word applied to me. I saw how He loved me and wanted the best for me. He did not desire that I should remain the same person; He wanted me to become the person He designed me to be.

As I got to know Jesus more intimately, I became unafraid to rid myself of bad habits and sins that hampered my relationship with Him and with others. I was honest with myself and desired to change to His image more than anything. He showed me where I needed to grow, and I gave Him time to work on me. Now, each day I ask Him to change me, show me, use me, and send me. He is faithful to bringing it to pass, in His time and in His way. I am His forevermore, and I look forward to what He will do for me and through me each and every day.

THE MASTER'S PROGRAM OF HIGHER EDUCATION

One of the greatest benefits of having a Daily Retreat is that we are taught by the master teacher Himself. What an education you are about to receive!

I was given a special revelation from the Lord about this fact in 2012 when my daughter was a sophomore at Metro State University in Denver, Colorado. It was August, and school was about to begin. I drove from my suburban home to downtown Denver to the university bookstore, where I met Susie. After gathering together her various books, we reached the cashier. At that point I proceeded to spend $465.98 on her hefty pile of biology, nutrition, sociology, and writing and research books. Ouch!

As I walked the mile back to the block where I had found a parking meter, I contemplated my own years of higher education and "Higher Education." I realized that my greatest learning had come through living life on a daily basis in my own uniquely designed master's program.

Spending time with my master instructor, Jesus, through reading the Holy Bible on a regular basis, was free of charge and endlessly applicable for me, semester after semester. In exchange for my myriad years at His feet, my teacher gave me the high marks of love, joy, peace, patience, kindness, goodness, faithfulness, gentleness, and self-control—marks that would endure unto eternity (Galatians 5:22–23 NIV).

You, too, may enroll in the "Master's Program of Higher Education." While the course is free of charge, there is still a price to pay. Just as time, hard work, dedication, and determination are required to complete any other college course, the same is true for the Master's Program.

Our lifelong learning begins when we open the greatest textbook ever written and apply the Word of God to our lives, one verse at a time, one day at a time. Our instructor beckons, "Call to Me and I will answer. I will tell you great and mighty things that you do not know" (Jeremiah 33:3 NIV).

As you receive His personal enlightenment on your Jesus journey, you will experience that His Word is a lamp unto your feet and a light unto your path (Psalm 119:105).

SPIRITUAL MANNA—MY DAILY SUSTENANCE

When the Israelites were enslaved by the Egyptians, they cried out to God for deliverance. God called Moses to the task of rescuing one million Jews via a mass exodus into the Sinai Desert (read the book of Exodus for all the miraculous details). You would think there would be joy and thankfulness. Instead, the Israelites complained because they didn't have the same delightful food that they'd eaten in Egypt as abused servants. Although God was fed up with their beefing, He patiently devised a plan for their desert nourishment, dreaming up a delicious wafer called manna, which tasted of coriander and honey.

> Then the Lord said to Moses, "I will rain down bread from heaven [called manna] for you. The people are to go out each day and gather enough for that day. (Exodus 16:4 NIV)

For forty years, the Israelites lived on manna, gathering just enough for each day.

In a similar way, I take in my own spiritual manna each morning, letting the Lord feed me with His bread from heaven. Each dawn, I look forward to ingesting His Word through the scriptures, receiving 100 percent of my recommended daily allowance of spiritual nutrition.

We've now prepped our minds for the journey, realizing that in the practice of Daily Retreat, we will be taught by our master teacher. Plus, we will take in considerable spiritual nutriments. Now, let's tweak our attitudes a bit to a God-pleasing state of being.

IT ALL BEGINS WITH "HERE I AM."

In 2001, a dear friend asked me to join her on the travel adventure of a lifetime. No, it wasn't an African safari or a trip to the outback of Australia. Instead, we went on a biblical dig, of sorts—reading the Bible chronologically all the way through in one year's time. That experience was life-changing.

One of the major impacts this fascinating immersion had on me was a brand-new awareness of a phrase spoken by a plethora of God-followers throughout biblical history. That phrase was "Here I am."

Those who responded to God's call with the words "here I am" included Abraham, Jacob, Moses, Samuel, David, Isaiah, and Jesus. I decided, then and there, that I, too, wanted to join the ranks of the here-I-am brigade.

In the same spirit of those who spoke those words two thousand to five thousand years ago, those who say these three words today are humble and ready to change bad habits for good ones, ugly attitudes for beautiful ones, complaints for thankfulness, and fear for trust.

The here-I-am folks are open-minded toward the wisdom of God and desire to be shown His new and improved ideas for effective living. Continually, the here-I-am followers obey what God the Father and Jesus, His Son, ask of them, knowing that individually they will be used to make a difference in their own spheres of influence. And ultimately, the here-I-am clan is willing to be sent anywhere or to do anything at any time for the "greater progress of the gospel" (Philippians 1:12 NIV).

Here is the proof that the appealing attitudes we are about to assimilate were the same ones practiced by incredible people of ginormous faith who were utterly available to God.

- Sometime later God tested Abraham. He said to him, "Abraham!" "Here I am," he replied. (Genesis 22:1 NIV)
- The angel of God said to me in the dream, "Jacob." I answered, "Here I am." (Genesis 31:11 NIV)
- So Moses thought, "I will go over and see this strange sight—why the bush does not burn up." When the Lord saw that he had gone over to look, God

called to him from within the bush, "Moses! Moses!" And Moses said, "Here I am." (Exodus 3:3–4 NIV)

- Then the Lord called Samuel. Samuel answered, "Here I am." (Samuel 3:4 NIV)
- Then I [David] said, "Here I am, I have come—it is written about me in the scroll. (Psalm 40:7 NIV)
- Then I [Isaiah] heard the voice of the Lord saying, "Whom shall I send? And who will go for us?" And I said, "Here I am. Send me!" (Isaiah 6:8 NIV)
- Here I am! I [Jesus] stand at the door and knock. If anyone hears my voice and opens the door, I will come in and eat with that person, and they with me. (Revelation 3:20 MSG)

Take a moment to ponder the following Daily Retreat Prayer, which I penned in 2001, when I pledged to God to join the here-I-am clan myself. Its purpose is to give the gift of a surrendered heart to God and thus receive His divine guidance for each day.

DAILY RETREAT PRAYER

Here I am in humility.
Change me.

Here I am in openness.
Show me.

Here I am in obedience.
Use me.

Here I am in willingness.
Send me.

REST STOP: HOMEWORK TIME

It's homework time again—time to get with Jesus and offer your life to Him in all sorts of new ways. If you will spend about twenty to thirty minutes with God over the next four to seven days, you will reap rich rewards in your reflection on the attitude and character traits He desires for you to have when meeting with Him. (From here on out, after each homework page, there will be a further reflection regarding that topic.)

As you take the exit to the rest stop, try praying the Daily Retreat Prayer. Enjoy becoming more enlightened regarding your one on one relationship with Jesus.

"HERE I AM" HOMEWORK DAY 1: MY HUMILITY; HIS CHANGES IN ME

Date:

1. Why does Father God want me to come before Him, first and foremost, in humility?

2. Why is humility also a way to be teachable?

3. What rewards are there for those with humility?

4. Why does Jesus want me to change if He loves me just as I am?

5. What advantages are there for me to change for the better?

6. How is the world a better place when I change for the better?

THE HUMILITY OF JESUS

Take a look at the definition of the word *humble* (www.dictionary.com):
hum·ble (adjective)

1. Not proud or arrogant, modest, a feeling of insignificance, inferiority, subservience
2. Low in rank, importance, status, quality
3. Courteously respectful

Do you and I consider ourselves to be humble? Of course, the question is a trick one we have all heard. If we say we are humble and act in humility, then we display our own pride. The correct answer is always no. In the area of humility, there is always room for improvement.

Our culture, however, is not one to promote much humility. Who wants to be low in rank? These days, who wants to be modest? How fun is it to have a feeling of insignificance? Seen this way, humility gets a very bad rap. Is there anything good about humility?

As we take our eyes off ourselves and place them on Jesus Christ, we see that, indeed, humility is the trait our Savior displayed in order to win us to the kingdom. The *American Tract Society Bible Dictionary* gives this definition of the word *humility*:

> humility
>
> The opposite of pride, in its nature and in the degree of its prevalence. It is often extolled in the Bible, (*Proverbs 15:33;16:19*), and the Savior especially exalts it *(Matthew 18:4)* and ennobles and endears it by his own example *(John 13:4–17, Philippians 2:5–8)*. Every created being, however holy, should possess it; but in the character of the sinful sons of men it should become a fundamental and all-pervading trait, to continue forever.[4]

Who can teach us humility except our submissive Lord Jesus Himself? As we study His life, words, and actions, we see that He alone is truly humble.

---

[4] (Authors/Editors unknown.) *The American Tract Society Bible Dictionary*. American Tract Society. New York: New Yorik. 1859.

Do nothing out of selfish ambition or vain conceit. Rather, in humility value others above yourselves, not looking to your own interests but each of you to the interests of the others. In your relationships with one another, have the same mindset as Christ Jesus: Who, being in very nature God, did not consider equality with God something to be used to his own advantage; rather, he made himself nothing by taking the very nature of a servant, being made in human likeness. And being found in appearance as a man, he humbled himself by becoming obedient to death—even death on a cross. Therefore God exalted him to the highest place and gave him the name that is above every name, that at the name of Jesus every knee should bow, in heaven and on earth and under the earth, and every tongue acknowledge that Jesus Christ is Lord, to the glory of God the Father. (Philippians 2:3–11 NIV)

Teach us, dear Savior, how to be like You. Amen.

"HERE I AM" HOMEWORK DAY 2: MY OPENNESS; HIS REVELATIONS TO ME

Date:

1. What does it mean to be open?

2. What is the difference between being open to God's ideas for me and being open to society's ideas for me? Why should God's ways take precedence?

3. What does it mean to be shown or to receive His revelation?

4. If I am open to being shown God's desires for me, what might occur?

5. God loves to reveal Himself to His faithful followers. How do I feel about His taking me into His confidence?

HOW TO MAKE A WISE DECISION

"Thar's gold in that there Good Book!" While financially I cannot rub two twenty-dollar bills together, spiritually, God's riches throughout His awe-inspiring Holy Bible are mine for the taking. The Lord showed me that I may use James 3:17 to discern whether a decision I make is wise or not:

> But the wisdom that comes from heaven is first of all pure; then peace-loving, considerate, submissive, full of mercy and good fruit, impartial and sincere. (NIV)

In making a wise and godly decision, I must see, first and foremost, if the action I may take is pure. Lest I forget what *pure* is, I can look in the Concordance (an alphabetical list of key words in the Bible, with scripture references as to verses containing that key word) in the back of my Bible under the word *pure*. Twenty-three verses are listed. One of those is Philippians 4:8:

> Finally, brothers and sisters, whatever is true, whatever is noble, whatever is right, whatever is pure, whatever is lovely, whatever is admirable—if anything is excellent or praiseworthy—think about such things. (NIV)

If what I am considering does not fit with being true, noble, right, lovely, or admirable, then it is not pure and would not be a godly or wise decision. Thus, it may be discarded from consideration.

If the subject matter *does* fit that list, then it can also be measured against the other conditions listed above—peace-loving, considerate, submissive, full of mercy and good fruit, impartial, and sincere.

If this is the case, then many of the decisions put before you or me (certain television programs, movies, other entertainment options, topics of conversation, financial expenditures, and so on) may not be wise. With guidance like this, spiritual wealth is ours to gain.

If your Bible does not have a Concordance, you may find a highly effective online concordance at BibleGateway.com. This site is a gold mine of information. Type the word *pure* in the search bar on the homepage, choose your Bible version (I use the New International Version, and there are many other choices), click the search bar, and you will see 104 verses that contain the word pure, including the two mentioned above.

Another tool to bank on! Happy discoveries and revelations are to come, which the Lord Himself will show you.

"HERE I AM" HOMEWORK DAY 3: MY OBEDIENCE; HIS USING ME

Date:

1. Why might *humility* and *openness* come before *obedience* in the Daily Retreat Prayer?

2. Why is obedience to Jesus a component of my loving Jesus?

3. Why does the word *obedience* have a bad connotation for some people? Is obedience difficult for you? If so, why?

4. When Jesus asks me to do something, how seriously will I take Him? How seriously does He want me to take Him?

5. Let me imagine some of the assignments Jesus might give me, reflecting on those that seem pleasant and those that are difficult. What gain will I receive in doing them, regardless of my preference?

6. To be used by Jesus is to be His extension to others. How might He use me in my own sphere of influence?

HAPPY USEFUL AND FRUITFUL DAY!

Each and every day may be deemed a holiday, called Useful and Fruitful Day, when we are used by God to make a difference in the lives of those around us. Peter describes how we affect the world.

> Make every effort to add to your faith goodness; and to goodness, knowledge; and to knowledge, self-control; and to self-control, perseverance; and to perseverance, godliness; and to godliness, mutual affection; and to mutual affection, love. (2 Peter 1:5–7 NIV)

As God develops these exceptional qualities in us (often through our individual experiences of difficulty, hardship, frustration, and so forth), we become useful to Him and fruitful for Him. When we display these colorful traits of Jesus to our families, friends, coworkers, and those we encounter in the community around us, His light is spread into many more corners.

Through our rainbow of surprising responses, we may label ourselves with Jesus's "Useful and Fruitful" stamp of approval as we bring His presence into the lives of others.

"HERE I AM" HOMEWORK DAY 4: MY WILLINGNESS; HIS SENDING OF ME

Date:

1. On a low to high scale from 1 to 10, where would I rate a heart that is willing to do what God wants that person to do? Why? What ranking do I give my own heart? Why?

2. What inner attitudes result from a willing heart?

3. How and why does Jesus take special care of His willing servants?

4. What is my attitude about being sent out by God on a new adventure?

5. Can I trust that I will be equipped to handle all new assignments that God gives to me? Why or why not?

THE COMPONENTS OF A GOD ASSIGNMENT

In Exodus 3, we see that God gave Moses an assignment: "Go tell Pharaoh to let My people go!" Wow! That's a heavy-duty assignment, and Moses was not too keen on being the one sent to do it. But God encouraged him, telling Moses that He would be with him every step of the way.

What assignments will God give to you and me? Are we ready to take them on, or will we balk, as Moses did? Here are the components of Moses's God-given assignment, as seen in Exodus 3, in order to better understand our own God assignments:

1. **God calls us to attention.**
   God called to him from within the bush, "Moses! Moses!" (Exodus 3:4)

2. **We stand ready.**
   And Moses said, "Here I am." (Exodus 3:4 NIV)

3. **God gives us our assignment.**
   So now, go. I am sending you to Pharaoh to bring my people the Israelites out of Egypt. (Exodus 3:10 NIV)

4. **We doubt our ability.**
   But Moses said to God, "Who am I that I should go to Pharaoh and bring the Israelites out of Egypt?" (Exodus 3:11 NIV)

5. **God reassures us of His capability.**
   And God said, "I will be with you." (Exodus 3:12 NIV)

6. **God tells us it will not be easy and to expect push-back, but He will see us through.**
   But I know that the king of Egypt will not let you go unless a mighty hand compels him … So I will stretch out my hand and strike the Egyptians with all the wonders that I will perform among them. After that, he will let you go. (Exodus 3:9, 20 NIV)

7. **God tells us that we will be victorious, gaining spiritual riches upon completion.**
   And I will make the Egyptians favorably disposed toward this people, so that when you leave you will not go empty-handed. (Exodus 3:21 NIV)

We are blessed when we accept God's assignments for our lives. Fear is natural, but God is fully capable. It's natural to resist and experience push-back, but with His help, we, like Moses, will be victorious.

I'm rooting for you to say yes to your many new God assignments!

PART 2

A NEW
APPROACH

Cindy and Leo, resting and enjoying the scenic overlook near the summit of Mount Bierstadt, Georgetown, Colorado

THE METHOD: SCRIPTURE REFLECTION

We have arrived at our first crossroads. We have begun this journey of understanding salvation, Jesus, and our own unique place in a one-on-one relationship with Him. We've also seen how our humble, prepared hearts will open up untraversed trails on this lifelong journey with our guide.

Up until now, with our homework, we have taken time to answer thought-provoking questions. Chapter 4, however, begins the new method of getting to know Jesus more intimately through reflecting on a verse of scripture each day, writing down a few thoughts on how the verse applies to our lives, and then asking God to help us live that out. If this is new or even scary, take heart and listen to what Jesus tells us right now:

> I will lead the blind by ways they have not known, along unfamiliar
> paths I will guide them; I will turn the darkness into light before them
> and make the rough places smooth. These are the things I will do; I will
> not forsake them. (Isaiah 42:16 NIV)

He's telling you, in essence, "I've got this, and thus, you've got this too." These uncharted paths will become well-traveled avenues soon enough. Eventually, you will find that, together, you and Jesus have paved a spiritual highway.

"NOW, I WILL TEACH YOU HOW TO HAVE A DAILY RETREAT"

When I first accepted Jesus as my Savior at age twenty-two, my husband and I lived in Greeley, Colorado, where he worked for a large construction company, and I was in my last year of college at the University of Northern Colorado. After much trial and error in church-hunting, we finally discovered a small, Bible-teaching fellowship on the outskirts of town. We had been attending only a short time when it was impressed upon me that the next step of faith I was to take was to be baptized.

Baptism, for the believer, is the outward expression of his or her inward belief in Jesus Christ's lordship. Unashamedly and publicly, the Christ-follower declares that Jesus Christ is Lord and Savior and will follow Him wherever He leads.

I was ready for this personal proclamation as Pastor Mike asked me why I wanted to be baptized. I declared, "I want to follow Jesus Christ for the rest of my life. I don't know where He will take me, but I am willing to take His hand and go along." I was quickly "plunged beneath the flood." Although I felt just the same, I arose a new creation.

Next, I was whisked away backstage, where the deaconesses were waiting with beach towels in hand to dry off Jesus's dewy, dripping disciples. A mom in early midlife, whom I did not know, blotted me and said with conviction, "Now, I'm going to teach you how to have a quiet time." This, I surmised, was the next step in the process of my new life in Christ. She invited me to her home for quiet-time lessons. I went with several other newbies to the faith and made a lifelong friendship with one of those women.

By inviting me to learn from her, quietly beautiful and obedient Barb did for me back in 1982 what I hope and pray to do for you right now—give you an everlasting practice that will benefit your life until you enter eternity. It is my sincere honor to invite you to learn the technique that has meant the world to me.

MY TRAVEL JOURNAL: RECORDING MY LIFE WITH GOD

Four of the first five books of the Bible, known as the Pentateuch by biblical scholars, cover the forty years that Israel wandered in the Sinai Desert under the guidance of God Himself. This meandering punishment was the result of the Israelites' lack of faith in God as protector and provider.

Thus, whenever I think of the Israelites wandering in the desert for forty years, it doesn't seem like much would have been accomplished, does it? Just the same old, same old—no growth, no progress. Yet in Numbers 33, Moses recorded the vast experiences of those forty years: miracles, hardships, refreshment, sadness, victory, and more.

Moses journaled his own life with God. Had he not written down these experiences, I might have falsely assumed that nothing much happened—that it was just forty wasted years of wandering.

I confess that sometimes I look at my own life this way too. I falsely assume that I haven't accomplished much. I wander about my house, day in and day out, doing laundry and loading the dishwasher. Lather, rinse, repeat!

Then I look at my own spiritual travel journal—the one in which I write during the week, recording what God is doing in my heart and mind. It is then I see God's faithfulness in bringing me through deserts; taking me to oases; showing me how to manage death, sadness, and difficulties; performing miracles for my benefit; and giving me victories to remember forever. I also see that, despite my forty years of circling through my kitchen and laundry room, I have indeed lived a life of progress. My spiritual journal is proof.

My hope is that you, too, will pull off life's superhighway to the scenic overlook and stop for a moment each day to reflect on your life with God. Record what you are going through and what God is teaching you. Day by day, you will see His faithfulness to you, His plan for you, and His successful deliverance of you into the promised land. After forty years, you will have no doubt but that you have traveled the distance with God.

The Scenic Overlook

I wonder how many hundreds of scenic overlooks I have whizzed by on the road due to my urgency to arrive more quickly at my destination. Yet each time I have taken the time to stop at a carefully chosen scenic overlook, I have been truly blessed by the glorious panorama. Developing the daily habit of looking over your life and assessing the view is an investment of time that will reap rich rewards.

The scenic overlook location: The place where you choose to have your Daily Retreat must be free from distraction. It should be comfortable and inviting (think bedroom, living room, study, kitchen table). This will be the place where you will be taught one-on-one by the Lord Jesus Christ. If possible, keep your Bible, pen, journal or notebook, and notepad in this place, ready for you to use as you begin each session. Do not begin other work simultaneously, such as checking your phone or starting a load of laundry. The enemy will use these "important" distractions to rob your time and to keep you from learning all that Jesus Himself desires to teach you. What place will you choose? Where was Jesus's preferred place?

> But Jesus Himself would often slip away to the wilderness to pray. (Luke 5:16 NASB)

When to pull over: For many, the best time to have their Daily Retreat is the first thing in the morning. With routines as they are, it will be easier to fit in rising earlier than squeezing in your Daily Retreat after you have begun your day, unless you have an empty slot of time at the same time every day (lunch, right after work when no one else is home, and so forth).

Another important reason to start your day with Daily Retreat is that the Lord will give you ideas of who you should call, speak to, or assist in some way. When the day is gone, so is the opportunity. For those whose time is best in the evening or late at night, put what you learn into practice the next day. What time of day works best for you—Psalm 119 or Psalm 16?

> I rise before dawn and cry for help, I have put my hope in Your Word. (Psalm 119:147 NIV)

> I will praise the Lord, who counsels me; even at night my heart instructs me. (Psalm 16:7 NIV)

How long to stay: Set aside fifteen to thirty minutes to be taught and to pray. Add five minutes to the front of your time slot to get ready and situated. If you rise twenty to thirty-five minutes earlier in the morning or forgo your favorite evening television program to do this, be assured that the Lord will notice and bless you for this sacrifice of time for His sake and yours. How much time can you give?

> For it is time to seek the Lord until He comes to rain righteousness on you. (Hosea 10:12 NASB)

DAILY RETREAT SUPPLIES

Before beginning your session, gather the following supplies together and put them in your scenic-overlook spot. A specially designated basket or tote is a nice way to have everything in one place.

Bible. The Word of God steers us in the right direction and keeps us on His path for our lives. A study Bible with notes at the bottom of each page is an excellent choice, as the insights will assist in bringing historical and contextual understanding. A laptop, tablet, or phone may also be used.

My personal practice and belief? There is a significant spiritual connection to holding, opening, reading, and highlighting your very own personal Bible. Which Bible version and format will you use?

> The words of the Lord are pure words; as silver tried in a furnace on the earth, refined seven times. (Psalm 12:6 NASB)

Highlighter or pencil. You will want to underline important, meaningful verses in your Bible. Over the years, these special verses will be there for you as you search for an encouraging word from the Lord or want to share a verse with someone else.

> Your Word is a lamp to my feet and a light to my path. (Psalm 119:105 NASB)

Journal or notebook. A journal or sturdy notebook will help you organize your thoughts and ideas in response to God's Word. Then you will have work to do (to change, to be shown, to be used, to be sent), and God will remember you, as you conform to His image, by blessing you. If you prefer, your laptop, tablet, or phone may also be used for this purpose. *Your Jesus Journey* book has appropriate space for your homework as well.

> Thus says the Lord, The God of Israel, "Write all the words which I have spoken to you in a book." (Jeremiah 30:2 NASB)

Notepad or to-do list. Things will pop into your head for you to get done that day (make a doctor appointment, get gas, wish Jill a happy birthday, take a sympathy card and plate of cookies to Rick). Jot these assignments down as they come to you, and continue on studying. Use this list to accomplish God's work for you that day.

> The plans of the diligent lead to advantage. (Proverbs 21:5a NASB)

DAILY RETREAT FORMAT

1. **Pray.** Tell God you are available to be taught by Him. "Here I am, Lord." In your journal, write a one-sentence opening prayer.

   > The Lord is good to those who wait for Him, to the person who seeks Him. (Lamentations 3:25 NASB)

2. **Read scripture.** Choose a passage or chapter to read. You may find a particular verse from this passage intrigues you; read the full paragraph surrounding the verse. As you read, ask God to help you understand what is being said and how it applies to your own life.

   > The Word of God is living and powerful and sharper than any double-edged sword piercing even to the division of soul and spirit, and of joints and marrow, and is a discerner of the thought and intents of the heart. (Hebrews 4:12 NASB)

3. **Choose a verse or passage from your reading and write it down.** This meaningful verse will be used to change, motivate, and transform your life, one day at a time.

   > All Scripture is inspired by God and profitable for teaching, for reproof, for correction, for training in righteousness, that the person of God may be adequate, equipped for every good work. (2 Timothy 3:16–17 NASB)

4. **Write a personal application about the verse for your life at that moment.** An open heart plus a willingness to change and act is all God needs to begin a mighty work in you.

   > For whatever was written in earlier times was written for our instruction, that through perseverance and encouragement of the Scriptures we might have hope. (Romans 15:4 NASB)

5. **Pray.** Be ready to implement what you have learned that very day. God often gives us the chance to practice what we were taught right away. Write a prayer about how you will use what you learned today. The prayer need not be long; one or two sentences often will be enough.

> Let the word of Christ richly dwell within you, with all wisdom. (Colossians 3:16a NASB)

6. **Write a title for the devotional you just created**. Put it at the top of your page. This is a brief synopsis of what you learned today from your time with the Lord. Here are some examples from my own Daily Retreat journal:

- Stand Firm
- Worry = Lack of Trust
- Live Joyfully
- Down with Double-Mindedness!

TRY ON A MINI-DAILY RETREAT FOR SIZE

Take a few minutes to try a sample Daily Retreat session, just to get the hang of it! Use the following verses from James 1:2–8 to get your feet wet. Here are the steps:

- Jot down the date.
- Pray the simple prayer listed.
- Read the passage from James.
- Reflect on it for a few moments.
- Choose one or maybe two verses.
- Write it down.
- Reflect on what the verse means for you personally.
- Write a few sentences about what God is revealing to you. Don't worry about spelling, grammar, or using full sentences. Just write what comes to your mind, as no one will read this but you.
- Write a one-sentence prayer about how you will implement your new learning.
- Give your Daily Retreat a title.

Let's try it now!

> [2] Consider it pure joy, my brothers and sisters, whenever you face trials of many kinds,
>
> [3] because you know that the testing of your faith produces perseverance.
>
> [4] Let perseverance finish its work so that you may be mature and complete, not lacking anything.
>
> [5] If any of you lacks wisdom, you should ask God, who gives generously to all without finding fault, and it will be given to you.
>
> [6] But when you ask, you must believe and not doubt, because the one who doubts is like a wave of the sea, blown and tossed by the wind.
>
> [7] That person [a doubter] should not expect to receive anything from the Lord.
>
> [8] Such a person [a doubter] is double-minded and unstable in all they do. (James 1:2–8 NIV)

DAILY RETREAT HOMEWORK PRACTICE WRITE

Date:

Title: (to be completed last)
Prayer: Here I am, Lord.
Passage: James 1:2–8

Verse(s):

Personal Application:

Prayer:

Title: (insert in space above)

YAY! YOU DID IT!

Congratulations on having personal time with the Lord via your Daily Retreat. How did you do? Did you have a new insight? How did you feel while doing this?

If this was hard or confusing for you, here is an example of a Daily Retreat I did. Remember, you will have your own questions, answers, and styles. My sister, who invites her counseling clients to write journals, always says, "No wrong; just write!"

CINDY'S DAILY RETREAT SAMPLE

Date: April 11, 2023
Title: *(to be filled in from below after the reflection time)* From Trepidation to Joy!
Passage: James 1:2–8 NIV

Verse: 2, Consider it pure joy whenever you face trials of any kind.

Personal Application: Hmmm. I have a trial right now, and it includes needing a larger sum of money than I have to pay an upcoming payment. When I think about this, the furthest thing from my mind is joy! How do I have joy when I feel extreme trepidation instead? If I were to replace that trepidation with joy, the only way to do it would be to *live by faith*. I ask You, Jesus, to show me how You and I can creatively make this payment and how I can trust You each time I begin to worry. Give me Your ideas and supply my needs (not my wants).

Prayer: Dear Jesus, let me turn my trepidation into joy because then I will see You work on my behalf. I give this dilemma to You. I trust You, and when I find myself not trusting You, let me reread James 1:2. Better yet, let me memorize it! In Your name I pray, amen.

Title: From Trepidation to Joy!

WE SERVE A GOD WHO ANSWERS THE SPIRITUAL CRIES OF OUR HEARTS

When I wrote that Daily Retreat sample while writing this book, it was a true cry of my heart. At that time, I knew I was going to publish this book through WestBow Press, but I had no idea how I was going to pay for it. God, in His love, provision, and confirmation, provided the *exact* amount needed, two months later, through an unexpected monetary check we received in the mail.

The gift was from an unknown life insurance policy from Leo's father and my father-in-law, John, who had passed away into glory in early May 2023. The total amount of the policy was divided evenly between his five children, and the surprise checks were disbursed in June 2023. Thanks to Dad's foresight some fifty years earlier, my husband's partnership with me throughout life, and Leo's personal investment in getting this book to you, *Your Jesus Journey* rests in your hands right now. Thank you, Father God, for this trio of provision, who could not have done it but for the giver or Giver who preceded him. Now that's a spiritual nugget to chew on!

Through the Daily Retreat process, I have lived by faith, trusting in God for my every need. I have seen scores of answers like this throughout my life. You, too, will experience individualized miracles from God.

DIFFICULTIES?

If you had difficulties in completing this sample or find that you struggle in any of the remaining homework assignments, please look over the Daily Retreat evaluation form for assistance—it is found after each section of homework. Also, there are online resources to help you. Find these in the "How to Use This Book" section at the beginning of this book. The goal is for you to experience success in this endeavor.

DAILY RETREAT EVALUATION FORM

1. **What worked for you?**

2. **What did not work for you? What was difficult? What needs to change?**

3. **Pray over the difficulties together with God.**

4. **What did you learn? How did the Lord speak to you or use you?**

5. **What excites you? What are your hopes?**

REST STOP: HOMEWORK TIME

We are now ready to begin another week of homework. This week, we will be reading in the book of James in the New Testament of your Bible. We will read a chapter a day for five days. Please choose and write down a verse that is meaningful to your current situation. Then, after reflecting on it, write a personal application, followed by a prayer and title.

Remember, the Lord Jesus has invited you to dine with Him and to partake of a spiritual meal. He has great and mighty words to whisper in your ear, as He knows all about you and your situation. At your chosen time and place, with your Bible and journal in hand, allow Jesus to reveal His insights for your life.

After each day of homework, you will find either a sample Daily Retreat for a guide or a reflection based on the verses in that particular chapter of James. These are to give encouragement as you incorporate the process of Daily Retreat into your daily routine.

It may take you more than five days to complete this homework if you have to skip a day in between. That is OK. Just complete the days as diligently as possible, and then return to chapter 5 when you are finished. May you feel the presence of Jesus with you as you apply the words of James to your life.

CHAPTER 4 HOMEWORK DAY 1: JAMES 1

Date:

Title: (insert at end of session)
Prayer: Here I am, Lord.
Passage: James 1

Verse(s):

Personal Application:

Prayer:

Title: (reinsert at top of page)

WHAT GOES IN MUST ALSO COME OUT: JAMES 1

Which verse(s) did you choose? How was your session with Jesus? He enjoyed your company; I know that for certain! Keep up the good work. You will experience inner transformation each day you spend time in this type of introspection.

Here's mine:

> **Verse:** Do not merely listen to the word, and so deceive yourselves. Do what it says … (James 1:22 NIV)

Personal Application: James tells me that when I ingest the Word of God, it should not remain inside of me in the "deep, stagnant pool of dead-end scripture." No, not on my living-water life! God's Word should not only be consumed, but it must also be lived out. As my heart changes on the inside, based on what I hear, read, and believingly incorporate, my actions toward my heavenly Father and others will then reflect my inner change.

Prayer: Lord Jesus, it does me no good to just ingest scripture and that's it. Your Word is supposed to propel me to action. I pray that I would do what you tell me to do in obedience. I will then be an active participant in living out scripture every day. Amen.

Title: What Goes in Must Also Come Out

CHAPTER 4 HOMEWORK DAY 2: JAMES 2

Date:

Title: (insert at end of session)
Prayer: Here I am, Lord.
Passage: James 2

Verse(s):

Personal Application:

Prayer:

Title: (reinsert at top of page)

BE A CONDUIT OF GOD'S LOVE IN YOUR DAILY LIFE: JAMES 2

What happened this time during your Daily Retreat? Each day of a Daily Retreat is different. Sometimes, I learn something new, or I might feel the urge to take a step of faith—stop worrying and believe God. Other days, I feel convicted—that there is something in my life that requires correction.

As an example, in my line of work as a home hospice certified nurse assistant, I am assigned to all sorts of homes and conditions within homes. The Lord Jesus was quick to show me that I had better not have preferences but instead treat all situations I encountered with equal love, respect, and service.

The verses I chose for this sample speak to this issue of playing favorites versus letting the love of Jesus flow out of me, whatever the circumstance.

Verse: If you show favoritism, you sin and are convicted by the law as a lawbreaker. For whoever keeps the whole law, but stumbles in one point is guilty of breaking it all ... Mercy triumphs over judgment. (James 2:9–10, 13b NIV)

Personal Application: My sin of favoritism and judgment will always clog up the works of God in my life. In the eyes of Jesus, every person is equally needy of His acceptance, love, and forgiveness. The gift of mercy, identifying with the hurt in someone else, will open the floodgates of compassion from my heart to theirs, as God uses me as a conduit of His love.

Prayer: Thank you, Lord, for never showing favoritism. All people are created by You to be promoted to Your kingdom. Forgive me for preferring some people or situations over others. May I see all people as You see them, beloved by You. I commit to being and sharing Your beautiful light with any person You put in my path. Amen.

Title: Be a Conduit of God's Love in My Daily Life

CHAPTER 4 HOMEWORK DAY 3: JAMES 3

Date:

Title: (insert at end of session)
Prayer: Here I am, Lord.
Passage: James 3

Verse(s):

Personal Application:

Prayer:

Title: (reinsert at top of page)

TWISTED-TONGUE SYNDROME: JAMES 3

When I was a young child, one of my favorite delights was going to the ice cream shop to get a soft-serve ice cream cone. The difficulty came in deciding which flavor to choose—chocolate or vanilla? Several years later, a genius inventor devised a machine that twisted both flavors together. A person could now enjoy both chocolate and vanilla in one bite. Heaven had come to earth in the form of the twist cone—splendidly blendable!

While the twisting of opposite ice cream flavors is delicious, James shows us that the twirly swirling of both praises and curses from our very own tongues to our God and to those made in His image, is quite distasteful indeed. Regarding our tongues, the loveliness of pure, sweet vanilla must prevail, while the darkness of chocolate criticism, complaints, and curses must diminish. From James 3:9–11 (NIV), we read:

> With the tongue we praise our Lord and Father, and with it we curse human beings, who have been made in God's likeness. Out of the same mouth come praise and cursing. My brothers and sisters, this should not be. Can both fresh water and saltwater flow from the same spring?

Twisted-tongue syndrome is an ugly reality for all of us on this side of heaven. With heightened awareness, however, and the help of our guide, the Holy Spirit, we may do battle to separate again what has been vilely twisted together in the same tongue.

Unitedly, let us long for purity of tongue, along with James and in honor of our heavenly Father.

CHAPTER 4 HOMEWORK DAY 4: JAMES 4

Date:

Title: (insert at end of session)
Prayer: Here I am, Lord.
Passage: James 4

Verse(s):

Personal Application:

Prayer:

Title: (reinsert at top of page)

THE REPENTANCE AND RESTORATION CYCLE: JAMES 4

After practice and a bit of time, you may feel free to be creative in your journaling. The Lord may give you an idea to draw a picture representing what you have read. Or you may want to make a list, chart, or diagram to show God's message.

> [7] Submit yourselves, then, to God. Resist the devil, and he will flee from you. [8] Come near to God and he will come near to you. Wash your hands, you sinners, and purify your hearts, you double-minded. [9] Grieve, mourn and wail. Change your laughter to mourning and your joy to gloom. [10] Humble yourselves before the Lord, and he will lift you up. (James 4:7–10 NIV)

As I sat with the Lord over this set of verses, I saw that they depicted what He and I call the Repentance and Restoration Cycle, found in myriad places throughout the Holy Bible and that we all need to put into practice on a regular basis. Here is a list I constructed for these verses, and next, a diagram I made in order to practically visualize scripture for our greatest benefit.

REPENTANCE AND RESTORATION GOD'S WAY

1. **Get with God.** ([7] Submit yourselves to God)
2. **Resist the temptation of Satan to *not* get with God.** ([7b] Resist the devil and he will flee from you.)
3. **Be ready to hear from God.** ([8a] Come near to God and He will come near to you.)
4. **Seek cleansing from sin and purification of mind.** ([8b] Wash your hands from sin [you sinners] and purify your hearts from double-mindedness [you double-minded]).
5. **Repent as necessary with one mind on the purpose.** ([9] Grieve, mourn, and wail. Change your laughter to mourning and your joy to gloom.)
6. **After such humility comes restoration and commission to go out again.** ([10] Humble yourselves before the Lord and He will lift you up.)

Following is my own diagram of this process. As you and I humble ourselves before God in sadness for the sin of which we have become aware, He forgives us and restores us. No more wallowing in self-pity or holding on to the crud in the camps of our hearts. No! God fully reinstates us to newness and sends us on our ways, serving Him once again as His beloved partners.

THE REPENTANCE AND RESTORATION CYCLE

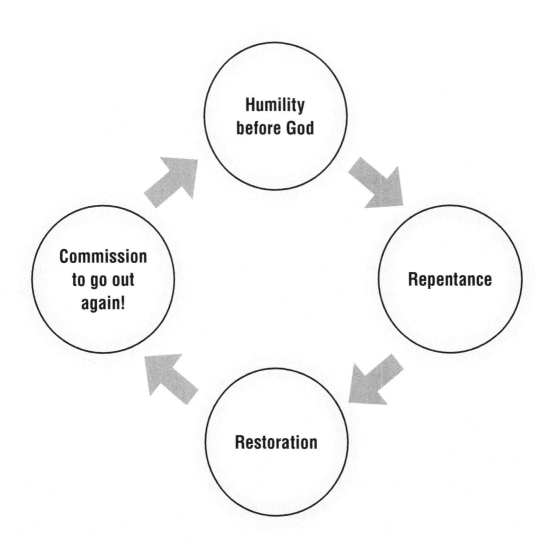

4 HOMEWORK DAY 5: JAMES 5

Date:
Title: (insert at end of session)
Prayer: Here I am, Lord.
Passage: James 5

Verse(s):

Personal Application:

Prayer:

Title: (reinsert at top of page)

ENDLESS PRAYER: JAMES 5

After you and I spend quality time with Jesus, how do we actually implement the teaching we've received into our lives? One way is by praying throughout the day.

> Is anyone among you in trouble? Let them pray. Is anyone happy? Let them sing songs of praise. Is anyone among you sick? Let them call the elders of the church to pray over them and anoint them with oil in the name of the Lord. And the prayer offered in faith will make the sick person well; the Lord will raise them up. If they have sinned, they will be forgiven. Therefore confess your sins to each other and pray for each other so that you may be healed. The prayer of a righteous person is powerful and effective. (James 5:13–16 NIV)

My response all day long, in every situation, is to pray and praise, conversing with God for protection, wisdom, guidance, right words, pleasant attitudes, help in times of trouble, ways to be effective in my work, and so on. Praising Him for His goodness, mercy, justice, compassion, sacrificial love, and much more additionally brings my mind into sync with His.

Such a prayer/praise lifestyle begets a closeness with Father God, Jesus Christ, and the Holy Spirit within us. These little, moment by moment prayers and praises, help to grow us up towards maturity, while pleasing and glorifying God who desires to be my Number One and yours!

May we believe that what we pray is powerful and effective. God hears our petitions and is thrilled when we practice endless prayer.

HOW DID IT GO?

I hope you got the hang of having a Daily Retreat during these past several days. My prayer is that it was helpful to you in some tangible way. Next, please find the Daily Retreat evaluation form to fill out, if desired, about your week of James homework. You may also go to "How to Use this Book" to find online answers to your questions.

DAILY RETREAT EVALUATION

1. **What worked for you?**

2. **What did not work for you? What was difficult? What needs to change?**

3. **Pray over the difficulties together with God.**

4. **What did you learn? How did the Lord speak to you or use you?**

5. **What excites you? What are your hopes?**

Trail to Bridal Veil Falls, Telluride, Colorado

5

THE REASON: WE NEED HIM DAILY

FIVE REASONS TO HAVE A DAILY RETREAT

You are now getting the hang of this journaling process called Daily Retreat. We get together with God, reflect on scripture, find a verse that has meaning for our current circumstances, write it down, write a personal application for the verse to change us in some way, pray about how the verse will affect our lives for the good, and finally, write a title for our time with the Lord that encapsulates the experience in a nutshell.

But why do any of this at all? Why go to the trouble, when we could just sleep in? Why is this practice so absolutely important?

Here are five reasons why having a Daily Retreat time with the Lord is so valuable:

1. We need a restored relationship with God.
2. We need daily rescue in the trials of life.
3. We need daily revelation (wisdom) for the decisions of life.
4. We need daily righteousness (conforming to the image of Jesus Christ, also known as sanctification).
5. We receive daily results (transformed thinking and acting).

In order to grasp the relevance of spending regular quality time with Jesus, let us look into each one of these principles individually.

REASON ONE: WE NEED A RESTORED RELATIONSHIP WITH GOD

How many times do we feel separated from God? We forget to pray, we forget to give thanks, we forget to remember that we are straying off His path for us. Daily Retreat offers a way to come back into alignment with God's guidance and grace.

In the Old Testament book of Jeremiah, God reminded His chosen people, the Jews, that they were forgetting all about Him in the business of their everyday lives.

> For My people have committed two evils: They have forsaken Me, the fountain of living waters to hew for themselves cisterns, broken cisterns that can hold no water. (Jeremiah 2:13 NASB)

Throughout the Old Testament, again and again, God urged His followers to acknowledge Him as Lord of their lives.

> "Thus says the Lord of hosts, 'Return to Me, that I may return to you.'" (Zechariah 1:3 NASB)

This same call of God to our own hearts requires a response. Without our own efforts to rebuild this broken bond, we remain separated from God too. Romans 3:23 (NIV) says, "For all have sinned and fall short of the glory of God."

When left to our own devices, all of us are unrighteous. None of us has a hope or a prayer, if this verse by itself is the end of the road. This impactful phrase, however, is sandwiched in between two even more amazing statements. Taken in this new context, there is absolute promise of restoration with God.

> *Righteousness is given by faith in Jesus Christ to all who believe. There is no difference between Jew and Gentile,* for all have sinned and fall short of the glory of God, *and all are justified freely by his grace through the redemption that came by Christ Jesus.* (Romans 3:22–24 NIV, italics added)

The flip side of the coin is that all are justified (made right with God) freely through the redemption that came by Jesus Christ. Just as all have sinned, so, too, any who believe are forgiven and deemed righteous.

You and I may enter into a restored relationship with God now, and well we should!

Let us then approach God's throne of grace with confidence, so that
we may receive mercy and find grace to help us in our time of need.
(Hebrews 4:16 NIV)

Wow! Thank you, Lord!

This good news is for you, for me, for our neighbors, for our communities, and
for our world. Any person may enter into a restored relationship with God by way of
Jesus Christ. Let us, then, pursue this relationship at all costs and by means of a Daily
Retreat with Him. Amen and amen!

REASON TWO: WE NEED DAILY RESCUE

Life often can be unbearably complex and demanding. In the midst of daily trials,
God is there to help us.

What problem looms in front of you today? The prophet Daniel, who, along with
most of his fellow Jews, was deported to Babylon as punishment for centuries of
forgetting about God, realized his nation's need of daily rescue:

All this disaster has come on us, yet we have not sought the favor of the
Lord our God by turning from our sins and giving attention to your
truth. (Daniel 9:13 NIV)

The prophet Isaiah knew that too much difficulty in a person's life would elicit a
cry for help as well.

When they cry out to the Lord because of their oppressors, he will send
them a savior and defender, and he will rescue them. (Isaiah 19:20b NIV)

After reading Genesis 37–50, all about the life of Joseph, I was amazed by the
many predicaments with which Joseph had to deal. Yet it is important to realize that
his crises were nearly identical to the troubles you and I deal with today: jealousy,
victimization, bad attitudes, temptations, waiting on God, cycles of life (prosperity
versus famine), forgiveness (giving and receiving it), fear of the unknown, and being
pushed out of his comfort zone. I don't know about you, but I can recognize many of
these dilemmas from my own experiences.

Here's the miracle: I have found that the greatest benefit of spending time with the
Lord on a regular basis is the personal assistance I get with the very real challenges
and celebrations of my one small life among eight billion on the planet. He has

become my wonderful counselor who encourages me and ministers to me in my struggles and victories.

When my family experienced an extended bout of unemployment during the financial crash of 2008, He said to me, "Cindy, it hasn't even been three years yet. Joseph experienced seven years of famine, and I provided for him through it all. I am waiting with you in God's waiting room, and that is enough. Come to Me, and I will give you rest. Smile because I am in control. Go forward with Me, one day at a time."

God is the same yesterday, today, and tomorrow. What He promised, He did—both for Joseph and for me. In Genesis 50:20a, Joseph told his brothers, "You meant evil against me, but God meant it for good" (NASB).

As you read and apply the Word of God to your own life, ask God to show you how you can trust Him to see good in the issues you face. God will bring about your preservation, just as He did for Joseph and his family. Come drink from the fountain of living water and be rescued and refreshed!

REASON THREE: WE NEED DAILY REVELATION (WISDOM)

We all want to make a difference in the world. As Christ-followers, we believe that God will use us for His purposes. Receiving daily revelation and wisdom from God's Word enables us to be discerning and to make right choices.

Moses (who, as you will recall, wandered in the Sinai Desert as the leader of a million grumbling Israelites for forty years) wrote these words of both warning and encouragement to you and to me:

> Teach us to number our days, that we may present to You a heart of wisdom. (Psalm 90:12 NASB)

James, as we saw in chapter 4, states plainly that you and I may simply ask God for this life-enhancing gift.

> If any of you lacks wisdom, you should ask God, who gives generously to all without finding fault, and it will be given to you. (James 1:5 NIV)

Finally, Jesus Himself, as a young teen, sought after His Father's wisdom:

> And Jesus grew in wisdom and stature, and in favor with God and man. (Luke 2:52 NIV)

The Holy Bible is the source of all wisdom. As we read and apply it regularly, it changes our perception, gives us knowledge, and creates a deep well of resourceful truth from which we can draw.

THE RICH WISDOM OF MEMORIZING AND KNOWING SCRIPTURE

I am a bit of a theatre geek. I fell in love with acting through my church youth group during my high school years, studied theatre in college, and have worked part-time as a children's theatre teacher for many years. As I had children, I loved to incorporate acting into our homeschool learning. When my oldest three daughters were ages eight, seven, and three, we memorized Psalm 1 together. The drama coach in me taught them hand motions to go with each phrase. Somehow, someone in my church got word of this and invited my daughters to recite Psalm 1 on stage during a worship service.

Their precious, pure children's voices, projecting loudly, rang out into the large sanctuary: "The Way of the Wicked versus the Way of the Righteous." They proceeded to recite beautifully the six verses of Psalm 1, convicting and captivating their adult audience with the truth and wisdom of the Word of God. Even years later, people commented on how those memorized scripture verses, resounding from the mouths of babes, had impacted their lives in a powerful way.

Fast forward to today, and I can testify that being in the Word of God on a day-by-day basis has solidified a plethora of scripture in my heart permanently. Perhaps I may not know the exact reference but because I have opened and read the Bible on a majority of my days on earth, I am able to share its truth with people I encounter.

My current call in life is as a certified nurse assistant, or CNA, working on a hospice team, ushering people into heaven. I was working with a patient one day and praying for this beloved new friend as I was about to leave his home. With my head bowed, I said, "Lord Jesus, You told Your disciples, 'I go to prepare a place for you. If it were not so I would have told you. I go, so that where I go, you may be also.' Lord Jesus, Horace and I are ready to see this beautiful new home You have prepared for us because we know that You are the way, the truth, and the life. We will gladly go whenever You come to take either of us to Your heavenly abode. Because of Your Resurrection and promise of eternal life when we believe, I pray this. Amen."

At the time I prayed that prayer with this dying gentleman, I was not racking my brain trying to remember which scripture I should repeat, nor did I spend any time thinking of what to pray ahead of time. Instead, the words and the scripture flowed out of my mouth, appropriately and Holy Spirit–driven, because of all the previous days and years I had spent with Jesus and His Word, intimately in my Daily Retreat time.

The drip, drip, drip of the Word of God in your heart and mine, over time, produces rich wisdom in your mind and mine, to bestow upon others when both we and they least expect it.

> My Father's house has many rooms; if that were not so, would I have told you that I am going there to prepare a place for you? And if I go and prepare a place for you, I will come back and take you to be with me that you also may be where I am. You know the way to the place where I am going." Thomas said to him, "Lord, we don't know where you are going, so how can we know the way?" Jesus answered, "I am the way and the truth and the life. No one comes to the Father except through me." (John 14:2–6 NIV)

REASON FOUR: WE NEED DAILY RIGHTEOUSNESS (CONFORMING TO THE IMAGE OF JESUS CHRIST)

In order to change from within, we must engage in honest self-examination. Daily Retreat allows us the opportunity to be conformed, in thought and in attitude, to the image of Jesus Christ over time, through God's supernatural power.

Paul talked about gaining a new, godly mindset in the book of Romans:

> Do not conform to the pattern of this world but be transformed by the renewing of your mind. Then you will be able to test and approve what God's will is—his good, pleasing and perfect will. (Romans 12:2 NIV)

But how does a person begin to think like Jesus? "I'm definitely not thinking like Him right now," you might say. "And what does reading the Bible have to do with anything?" As we experienced firsthand in the James homework in chapter 4, scripture can be used to correct and rebuke us. God wants to sanctify us and often uses a bit of discipline to do so. Sanctification, or becoming more righteous, is God taking the ugly parts of our inner beings and making them beautiful. God's greatest desire after we say yes to Him is then to conform us into the image of His Son, Jesus.

Thus, God desires that the negative parts of our personalities, along with our bad habits and unrighteous thoughts, be worked on (to put it mildly). He is always a gentleman about it but will spare no expense to pull us off the wide road that leads to destruction and send us, instead, through the narrow gate that leads to life.

Such direction toward righteousness often involves His rebuke—or what I have fondly termed throughout my life as a "swift kick in the rear"! These kicks are spiritual, but I promise that I feel them as if they were real. When I get one, I move; you can be certain. God doesn't mess around and doesn't desire that I mess around any longer either.

One such kick in the rear I received was in preparation of finally putting this book together. I had no clue that the time was approaching; I only knew that I had a book inside of me, plus partially in front of me, and one day, I would write it.

One morning in the fall of 2022, Jesus impressed upon me that there were people out there who needed a deeper relationship with Him. He urged me to teach my Daily Retreat class beginning in January 2023 at my beloved church fellowship for some particular people He had chosen. I considered it and said, "Sure, I can do that." A few days went by, however, without my pursuing it further.

Several mornings later, in our Daily Retreat time, I got the kick—ouch!—and I mean yowie! You can bet that I called Pastor Nathan that very day and said, "I need to have a meeting with you about teaching a Sunday school class in January."

His reply? "Wow, we were just looking for someone to teach a Sunday school class in January! What's your topic?"

Throughout my life, I have learned that getting kicked in the rear isn't so bad. It wakes me up to my thinking and acting and how I very much need to monitor it. The sanctification process, or receiving more of the righteousness of Jesus Christ, our Savior, is all about close inspection of our behavior through the urging of the Holy Spirit, to make our attitudes and conduct more pleasing to Jesus and Father God.

Thank you for your willingness to be kicked in the rear along with me, in order to slowly but surely be transformed into the likeness of Jesus Christ.

REASON FIVE: WE RECEIVE DAILY RESULTS

Spending time with the Lord in prayer and introspection brings blessings to our lives: the Holy Spirit flowing within us, a fruitful existence, and victorious living in good times and bad.

A daily dose of scripture and time with Jesus turns the fire of the Holy Spirit within us up to full blast! It's a far cry from quenching the Spirit; instead, we receive His holy guidance and power throughout our days.

> May the God of hope fill you with all joy and peace as you trust in him,
> so that you may overflow with hope by the power of the Holy Spirit.
> (Romans 15:13 NIV)

Fruitful living enlivens our days as we see that we are being used by God to accomplish His purposes, insofar as we are each connected firmly to the Vine, who is our friend, Jesus.

> "I am the vine; you are the branches. If you remain in me and I in you, you will bear much fruit; apart from me you can do nothing." (John 15:5 NIV)

And who wouldn't get excited about the many victories we receive from our close walk with Christ?

> But thanks be to God! He gives us the victory through our Lord Jesus Christ. (1 Corinthians 15:57 NIV)

MISSION: POSSIBLE! FROM TEMPTATION TO VICTORY IN A WILDERNESS EXPERIENCE

Did you ever watch reruns of the 1960s television show *Mission: Impossible*? Instructions for conquering the impossible tasks were given to the hero via a taped recording, which then self-destructed. He had to hear it right the first time or else! We, too, may find ourselves with an impossible set of circumstances with little or no instruction on how to deal with the overwhelming battle ahead.

Jesus Himself was faced with quite an impossible assignment, one in which He possibly could fail or experience victory, based on His reliance on the Holy Spirit. And by the way, He passed the test with an A+++.

> Jesus, full of the Holy Spirit, left the Jordan and was led by the Spirit into the wilderness, where for forty days he was tempted by the devil. He ate nothing during those days, and at the end of them he was hungry. (Luke 4:1–2)

Satan, of course, was present at Jesus's weakest point, when He was physically spent and exhausted. He told Jesus to feed Himself miraculously, rather than rely on God. Satan offered an emotional solution to Jesus's impossible mission, telling Jesus that he would give Jesus the things God was not yet giving Him. He also offered a false spiritual solution, asking Him to test God to see if He was real.

In this seemingly impossible mission, Jesus relied on the Holy Spirit within and the Word of God without to thwart the schemes and lies of Satan. His (summarized) responses were:

- People live best under the care and direction of God. He promises to care for me, and I believe it, regardless of this wilderness experience.
- Worship God alone, submitting to His plan, whether or not any other worldly benefits are received.
- Trust God fully, no matter what difficulties are faced. Give God full charge.

In our own wilderness experiences and difficult times, you and I can be certain that Satan will try to trip us up too with his lies and schemes. In his nasty dealings with Jesus, Satan saw that he had no power over the Word of God or the one using it, and he left. Victory is ours when, like Jesus, we rely on both the Holy Spirit and the Word of God, which never self-destruct and are valid truths for yesterday, today, and tomorrow.

Know now that resisting the devil causes him to flee. Therefore, may you and I experience victories in the "wilderness" through reliance on Jesus Christ, the Holy Spirit, and the truth of God's Word. These, then, are the daily results we can take to the bank.

REST STOP: HOMEWORK TIME

Now that you know five excellent reasons to have a Daily Retreat, let's dive into another five days of homework. This session, our focus is on the psalms, found about two-thirds of the way through the Old Testament. The themes of the chosen psalms coincide with the themes of the five reasons to have a Daily Retreat. Here is a bit of background on these readings.

- Psalm 51, which focuses on repentance and restoration, was written by King David after he committed the sins of adultery and murder.
- Psalm 91, written by Moses, is a wonderful depiction of God's care for His own and conveys the theme of rescue.
- Psalm 1 shows the prudence of choosing the right path, with its theme of revelation and wisdom.
- The theme of righteousness (or sanctification) is found in Psalm 146 in the attitude of praise in all circumstances and being like Jesus in loving the underdog.
- Finally, Psalm 128 relays the point of results, as the follower of the Lord experiences God's blessing and goodness.

After each day of homework, a commentary follows.

Ideally, if you can complete these five Daily Retreat sessions within a seven-day period, that would be great. Perhaps you will need ten days to complete the five-day homework assignment, doing one every other day. That is perfectly fine. Please stay interested and accomplish what you are able to do.

The point is, do not get discouraged! Complete what you can, and then return for more of His blessings. If you've wrestled with the homework, fill out the Daily Retreat evaluation form. You may also find out how to get online help in the "How to Use this Book" section.

Thank you for your participation and for allowing God to bring you restoration, rescue, revelation, righteousness, and results in your life this week. Enjoy personal, you-focused time with Jesus, who loves you and wants to supply to you exactly what you need.

CHAPTER 5 HOMEWORK DAY 1: PSALM 51

Date:

Theme: Restored Relationship with God
Title: (insert at end of session)
Prayer: Here I am, Lord. Restore in me a right relationship with You, and thank you!
Passage: Psalm 51

Verse(s):

Personal Application:

Prayer:

Title: (reinsert at top of page)

Rejoicing in Rubbish Removal

Where are you on Thursday mornings at seven o'clock? As my neighbors will attest, I am often found running down the street, chasing after the trash truck, flailing my arms and screaming at the top of my lungs, "Stop! Stop! Please come back! Hey! Wait up!" I finally catch their attention half a block down the road.

As I approach them, the three strong young men in the truck watch as I wildly explain to them—in sign and body language—that I need them to turn their truck around and go back to my house, where my stinky, full trash cans have just been placed at the curb because I forgot (again) to put them out last night. "Please, please, would you mind going back?"

One young man rolls his eyes at my embarrassing appearance. The second mumbles words I cannot translate. They defer to the driver, who, sizing me up in my pajamas and gym shoes, kindly replies, "OK. We'll be back." He remembers me and knows that I will have three sodas and three granola bars waiting for them.

This pattern worked out fairly well for me over the years—until two months ago, when I was just a bit later to realize my mistake, and my trash was just a bit heavier to drag to the street on such short notice. Also, I couldn't find my gym shoes. I grabbed a pair of my daughter's larger flip-flops and took off again, yelling and hollering the familiar words, "Stop, please, wait, come back!" Sadly, it was to no avail. The truck rounded the bend, heading toward busy Ward Road.

As I walked back to my house, I could not help but notice the empty, fresh cans belonging to each of my neighbors. Their containers were free of trash and debris, standing ready for the new week ahead. I could see mine in the distance, overflowing with white plastic bags and surrounded by large black bags filled with weeds and grass clippings.

Because of the one-hundred-degree days, I could almost distinguish the putrid fumes from last week's leftovers rising from the can into the sun. It would be a long, long week ahead. Why, oh, why was I so forgetful? It would now be impossible to sit out on the back patio and enjoy the summer evenings. Oh, woe was me, with the burden of bags of rubbish!

A thought crossed my mind. I could phone the company and ask them to return. It would be well worth the price to pay. I found the number and called. "I forgot to put my trash out this morning and missed your truck. Could you send another one out? You will? May I ask how much that will cost? Free?"—it was a courtesy because I was a faithful customer. Someone would be there within the hour. "Oh, thank you, thank you so much. I am truly grateful."

With soda and granola bar in hand, I presented them to the courtesy driver. "Thank you, thank you for taking my stinky trash away!"

Smiling, he replied, "It's my job. You'll never have to smell it again!"

After reading Psalm 51 this week, let us rejoice, knowing our rubbish has been removed for good. We are clean, free, restored, standing tall, smelling fresh, and completely ready to move forward toward the Son in the upward call of Christ.

CHAPTER 5 HOMEWORK DAY 2: PSALM 91

Date:

Theme: Rescue
Title: (insert at end of session)
Prayer: Here I am, Lord. Rescue me today and show me Yourself!
Passage: Psalm 91

Verse(s):

Personal Application:

Prayer:

Title: (reinsert at top of page)

DWELLING IN THE FORTRESS

My lovely mother-in-law, Marianne, lived life as a young child in Bergstadt-Platten, Germany, during World War II. When Marianne was ten years old, the war ended. The national boundaries were redrawn, and Bergstadt-Platten became a part of Czechoslovakia. The Germans who lived there, including my mother-in-law's family, were ordered onto railroad cars and sent to unknown destinations back west into Germany. After several stops, Marianne's family was assigned to live in an apartment in a castle for a year while Germany was in the cleanup process.

Imagine the fear that must have gripped Marianne in her childhood with the horror of war surrounding her. Then, what relief she must have felt to be placed in the shelter of a castle, a fortress designed to safeguard all who dwelled inside from the encircling enemy. I surmise she eventually felt free enough to play within its walls, laugh again, and live as a child is designed to live—cared for and protected.

As I sat with the Lord, meditating on Psalm 91, I became aware that He is my castle and longs for me to take refuge in Him daily. Even though my house is in Colorado, my dwelling place is in the "shelter of the Most High; my refuge and my fortress, my God, in whom I trust" (Psalm 91:1–2 NIV).

As you and I seek to dwell with God, our refuge, shield, and bulwark, He promises to answer when we call, to be with us in trouble, and to rescue us, honor us, and satisfy us so that we might behold His salvation.

Run to the fortress! Be certain of the protection that is yours because you have known His name. You are now set securely on high.

CHAPTER 5 HOMEWORK DAY 3: PSALM 1

Date:

Theme: Revelation (Wisdom)
Title: (insert at end of session)
Prayer: Here I am, Lord. Give me greater wisdom from You today.
Passage: Psalm 1

Verse(s):

Personal Application:

Prayer:

Title: (reinsert at top of page)

"GIVE ME SPIRITUAL WISDOM AND KNOWLEDGE"

In 1 Kings 3:5, God tells Solomon to ask Him for any gift Solomon would like. God said, "Ask for whatever you want me to give you" (NIV).

Wow, how would you answer that question? "A new car!" or "A trip around the world!"

Solomon responded in 1 Kings 3:9 (NIV), "Give your servant a discerning heart to govern your people and to distinguish between right and wrong."

Second Chronicles 1:10 (NIV) records Solomon as saying, "Give me wisdom and knowledge, that I may lead this people, for who is able to govern this great people of yours?"

God was pleased and answered his request.

> God gave Solomon wisdom and very great insight, and a breadth of understanding as measureless as the sand on the seashore. (1 Kings 4:29 NIV)

As I reflected on this request and God's answer, I wondered if you and I have ever asked God to give us spiritual wisdom and knowledge. How valuable to have a spiritually discerning heart, to see God everywhere in our lives, and to know His will for us, each and every day.

As you and I bathe in His Word and seek personal change, which shapes us into the image of Christ, spiritual-heart cell by spiritual-heart cell, we undoubtedly will gain measureless spiritual wisdom and knowledge. Thanks be to God for the changes that have already occurred in your heart and mine.

After reading Psalm 1, you and I may wisely discern between the paths to take in life—the one that leads to life eternal or the one that eventually leads to destruction. Let us be fruitful trees, planted firmly by the living water of Jesus Christ!

Like King Solomon, let us ask for greater spiritual wisdom, revelation, and knowledge from our God, who longs to give us His good gift of spiritual insight.

CHAPTER 5 HOMEWORK DAY 4: PSALM 146

Date:

Theme: Righteousness (conforming to the image of Christ, or sanctification)
Title: (insert at end of session)
Prayer: Here I am, Lord. Let me be the hands and feet of Jesus, in thankfulness.
Passage: Psalm 146

Verse(s):

Personal Application:

Prayer:

Title: (reinsert at top of page)

THE UNDERSTOOD YOU: PRAISE THE LORD!

One of my favorite subjects as a middle-schooler was language arts. Parts of speech and grammar took on life and excitement as my delightful teacher, Mrs. Johnson, taught us about the structure of the English language. One lesson was learning how to find the subject and verb of a sentence, such as, *Jack rides around town in the car with Mom.* First, we were to cross out all prepositional phrases: *around town, in the car,* and *with Mom.* Next, we were to find the verb, or action, word: *rides.* Finally, we were to find the subject—who or what did the action: *Jack.*

After becoming proficient at this, an interesting sentence came my way: *Sweep the cobwebs with the broom.* I crossed out the prepositional phrase: *with the broom.* I found the verb: *sweep.* But where was the subject? Was the subject "cobwebs"? Cobwebs don't sweep!

With a twinkle in her eye, Mrs. Johnson smiled and told us the secret. The sentence was a command, and the subject was the "understood you." We were to put the subject *You* before the sentence like this: *(You) Sweep the cobwebs with the broom.* How excited I was to find another command sentence so I could put "(You)," (which was really me) as the subject!

Psalm 146 is also a command, with the verb being *Praise* and the subject being the understood you (or more importantly, the understood me). I am commanded to "Praise the Lord," yesterday, today, tomorrow, and forever—no ifs or buts about it!

When my son Jack was thirteen, he spent a day riding 120 miles in the car with me. As we pulled into the driveway, he commented, "You sure complain a lot, Mom." Since I consider myself to be an upbeat person, and I had vowed, along with David, not to sin with my mouth—"Set a guard, O Lord, over my mouth. Keep watch over the door of my lips" (Psalm 141:3 NIV)—I said, "I do?"

He proceeded to repeat phrases I had said throughout the day concerning other people's driving. "It's a good thing I'm here with you instead of one of your friends."

Ouch! Over the years, as a follower of the Lord, I have learned to expect and accept a swift kick in the rear from God now and then in whatever way He desires to admonish me—this time by using Jack's observations. The "understood me" realized I had failed to praise the Lord, as adjured by the psalmist.

Forgive me, Lord. Forgive me, Jack. Forgive me, drivers. Praise the Lord that we weren't in an accident. Praise the Lord that we reached our destinations safely. Praise the Lord that He is the God of second, third, and thirty-thousandth chances! Praise the Lord that He loves me enough to show me where I fail. Praise the Lord that I am willing and ready to be shown my certain shortcomings. Praise the Lord that I can regroup and refocus so that all my breaths are filled with praise. Praise the Lord for Mrs. Johnson, who taught me that *I* am the subject of the command, "Praise the Lord!"

CHAPTER 5 HOMEWORK DAY 5: PSALM 128

Date:

Theme: Results
Title: (insert at end of session)
Prayer: Here I am, Lord. May I experience blessing and goodness from Your hand.
Passage: Psalm 128

Verse(s):

Personal Application:

Prayer:

Title: (reinsert at top of page)

THE GOOD LIFE VERSUS THE BLESSED LIFE

In the American dream story, the goal is to live the good life, isn't it? The hope in society is for a high-paying job (or at least a credit card in our wallets), an accumulation of many toys, and thus the ability to kick back and enjoy a life of leisure. This mindset, however, usually results in feelings of pride and entitlement because "I did it my way," as the 1940s crooner Frank Sinatra vocalized.

Not long ago, I saw this very mentality played out on a license plate. I was stopped at a red light behind a high-end sports utility vehicle with a license plate that read, U12BME—translated as "You want to be me." Hmmm. At that moment, did I wish to be that driver? Well, I can say that Satan, in his sly, alluring enticements, wanted me to wish it. He wanted me to feel that my low-end, efficient-mileage vehicle was somehow not enough—that I should wish for more. After all, I live in America.

Conversely, the good Lord desires to give us a blessed life. In exchange for His marvelous gifts, He requires simply that you and I revere Him and then lead an obedient lifestyle, following His guidelines given to us in scripture:

> Blessed are all who fear the Lord, who walk in obedience to him. (Psalm 128:1 NIV)

This psalm goes on to say that these are the blessings that come from such a lifestyle:

1. Our lives will be fruitful (Psalm 128:2), from our godly work and dedication to our Father.
2. We will live in prosperity (Psalm 128:2). Although I am not rich like the U12BME driver, I am blessed with health, contentment, and lack of strife. You may have those or different blessings of prosperity here on earth. And we all will be much more than prosperous in our lives in heaven.
3. Our families will be blessed (Psalm 128:3).
4. We may be given a long life by which to enjoy our grandchildren (Psalm 128:6).

Psalm 128:5a (NIV) says, "May the Lord bless you from Zion." Zion is both another name for Jerusalem, the Lord's city, and a reference to His heavenly kingdom. So then, let us praise God, from whom all blessings flow out from His heavenly home, Zion, to His beloved followers here on earth below. Amen.

DAILY RETREAT EVALUATION

1. **What worked for you?**

2. **What did not work for you? What was difficult? What needs to change?**

3. **Pray over the difficulties together with God.**

4. **What did you learn? How did the Lord speak to you or use you?**

5. **What excites you? What are your hopes?**

PRAYING HANDS TRAIL, NEAR APACHE JUNCTION, ARIZONA

6

CONQUERING ROADBLOCKS

Temptation: Flat Tire or Fully Inflated?

Chapter 5 showed us why we should spend high-quality time with Jesus. Those five sensible facts fill up our gas tanks and fuel our desire for this Jesus journey. But now, in chapter 6, we need to slow down and evaluate the journey thus far. How has it been going for you? Has traveling been a breeze, with the Daily Retreat time coming along easily? If so, congratulations. You have discovered how to fit this new cadence into your weekly routine.

If this does not describe you, you have most likely experienced a flat tire or two along the way. There's nothing like that deflated feeling, is there? It dawns on us that we are now totally out of alignment! Trying to push something new into an already hectic life is not working out. Why is this process of pursuing time with Jesus *so* difficult? Nothing is happening as we had hoped.

The good news is that all is not lost—far, far from it. We are about to inch over to the shoulder of the thoroughfare to examine some of the roadblocks that prevent success in this endeavor. These roadblocks, or setbacks, can also be termed "temptations."

Our adversary the devil prowls around, seeking any he might prevent from taking on this very challenging and life-enhancing practice that you have chosen to embrace. "Why should you travel the road to success?" your archenemy wonders. "No way. It's high time to puncture a tire or set up a construction zone! Stall-outs are my specialty."

But the apostle Paul, writing to the believers in Corinth, gave them (and us) the key to success when it came to ensnarement in the devil's schemes.

> No temptation has overtaken you except what is common to mankind. And God is faithful; he will not let you be tempted beyond what you can bear. But when you are tempted, he will also provide a way out so that you can endure it. (1 Corinthians 10:13 NIV)

God is faithful to help us steer clear from temptation's deep potholes. Let's change that flat to a brand-new all-season radial that will weather all the challenges of the turnpike ahead.

FIVE ROADBLOCKS TO A DAILY RETREAT

Here are five hazards our adversary would like to employ against us on the road to progress:

1. Lack of a routine or practice
2. Lack of self-discipline
3. The belief that we are too busy for a daily retreat
4. The belief that we do not really need a daily retreat
5. Unwillingness to face God's truth or guidance for us

Are any of these roadblocks stalling you out? If so, pinpoint and then confess the difficulty to God. He will help you overcome whatever impedes your advancement.

ROADBLOCK ONE: LACK OF A ROUTINE OR PRACTICE

Consistency is the key to consecutive days with Jesus. It may take several weeks or months of plugging away until this becomes a normal routine. In our world of instant satisfaction, it seems a laborious undertaking to have to keep at something so persistently until we finally figure out what works best. Yet truthfully, there is time to slow down at this juncture. We have our whole lives to get to our ultimate destination.

Perhaps you could try just two Daily Retreats per week. Maybe early on a Saturday and Sunday morning would work, when no one else is up, and it is just you and Jesus. Why not commit to spending one year with the Lord in developing this lifelong habit together, trying various plans until you land on the right one?

> Commit to the Lord whatever you do, and he will establish your plans.
> (Proverbs 16:3 NIV)

Ask, seek, and knock on heaven's door to get personal attention and help in this matter. I know you will receive an answer to this type of wholesome request.

INCREASING IN SPIRITUAL SIGHT

As you and I plug away at the practice of scripture reflection, day after day after day, we will begin to notice that our spiritual sight increases. Contemplate this account of a blind man, healed by Jesus, and his gradual accrual of ocular perception.

> They came to Bethsaida, and some people brought a blind man and begged Jesus to touch him. He took the blind man by the hand and led him outside the village. When he had spit on the man's eyes and put his hands on him, Jesus asked, "Do you see anything?"
>
> He looked up and said, "I see people; they look like trees walking around."
>
> Once more Jesus put his hands on the man's eyes. Then his eyes were opened, his sight was restored, and he saw everything clearly. (Mark 8:22–25 NIV)

You and I grow in spiritual insight with practice and a set routine. While learning, we understand a little; then, with time and focus on Jesus Christ, as with the blind man, we gain clearer vision of exactly who is directing our steps.

What is your story? When were you blind? How did Jesus give you spiritual sight? Have you continued to increase in your understanding of Jesus and His teachings, or are they still a bit obscured and indistinct?

In time, we will be like the disciple Peter, who gained greater spiritual sight with the more time he spent with Jesus.

> "But what about you [disciples]?" Jesus asked. "Who do you say I am?"
>
> Simon Peter answered, "You are the Messiah, the Son of the living God."
>
> Jesus replied, "Blessed are you, Simon, son of Jonah, for this was not revealed to you by flesh and blood, but by my Father in heaven. And I tell you that you are Peter and on this rock, I will build my church, and the gates of Hades will not overcome it." (Matthew 16:15–18 NIV)

With practice and a routine, our reward will be greater spiritual sight to clearly see the important messages Jesus has for you and me, individually.

ROADBLOCK TWO: LACK OF SELF-DISCIPLINE

It is our natural tendency to take the easy way out, such as sleeping in, checking our phones, or starting work or housework before we meet with the Lord. Then, the time is gone before we know it. Likewise, when the time-for-Daily-Retreat alarm rings and pressing *snooze* is our best response, we rob ourselves of growth and life.

The Bible itself gives us swift kicks in the rear, as does God. In the book of Proverbs in the Old Testament, King Solomon, with his gift of wisdom, admonishes you and me when we have a sluggard's mentality.

> Go to the ant, you sluggard; consider its ways and be wise! It has no commander, no overseer or ruler, yet it stores its provisions in summer and gathers its food at harvest. How long will you lie there, you sluggard? When will you get up from your sleep? (Proverbs 6:6–9 NIV)

The writer of Hebrews in the New Testament also denounces laziness and promotes discipline:

> We do not want you to become lazy, but to imitate those who through faith and patience inherit what has been promised. (Hebrews 6:12 NIV)

> No discipline seems pleasant at the time, but painful. Later on, however, it produces a harvest of righteousness and peace for those who have been trained by it. (Hebrews 12:11 NIV)

Contrary to lethargic procrastinators, the rewards of the diligent and disciplined will be great. Jesus appreciates when you and I show effort to be with Him. He promises to make our time with Him profitable.

> Listen to advice and accept discipline, and at the end you will be counted among the wise. (Proverbs 19:20 NIV)

MY OWN REFORM SCHOOL

Some years ago, my three youngest children were blessed to attend a local charter school that based its philosophy of education on the "love and logic" work of Jim Fay and Foster Cline, MD,[5] teaching students to be responsible for their own choices.

---

[5] https://www.loveandlogic.com/pages/about, Accessed December 18, 2023.

At one parent/teacher/student conference, my twelve-year-old son's science teacher said to him, "If you don't like the grade you are receiving, you will need to change something up. Perhaps you need to move to the empty table away from certain students, or maybe you need to come in after school for tutoring. This grade you consider undesirable will certainly stay the same until you implement a change of thinking about your studies."

Wow! I realized that I, too, was implementing my own change in thinking through "Jesus's Reform School" of my mind! My own undesirable traits and practices required a reform in thinking and action so that I could attain a more desirable outcome. And from who better to receive instruction on life through an alteration in perception than Jesus Christ Himself? The Gospels are chock-full of Jesus's advice on replacing one way of thinking with another to get a more "abundant life" return. How about this one from Matthew 5?

> "You have heard that it was said to the people long ago, 'You shall not murder, and anyone who murders will be subject to judgment.' But I tell you that anyone who is angry with a brother or sister will be subject to judgment. Again, anyone who says to a brother or sister, 'Raca,' [an Aramaic word of insult] is answerable to the court. And anyone who says, 'You fool!' will be in danger of the fire of hell. (Matthew 5:21–22 NIV)

As you and I spend time with the master teacher Himself each day, let us desire to enroll in His personalized "reform school," which will enhance our lives and help us through the ups and downs. His unconventional advice for true fulfillment is worth every change we make. Seclude with Jesus today, and experience the transformed frame of mind He bestows upon the industrious.

ROADBLOCK THREE: THE BELIEF THAT WE ARE TOO BUSY FOR A DAILY RETREAT

So many of us have so much to do in a day. We have arduous jobs, children who must be transported here and there, responsibilities as family members, and all of the day-to-day household tasks that are ever before us. Doesn't busyness like this count for something?

Hmmm. God says we should still make time for Him.

> "You refuse to listen when I call and no one pays attention when I stretch out my hand." (Proverbs 1:24 NIV)

"You expected much, but see, it turned out to be little. What you brought home, I blew away. Why?" declares the Lord Almighty. "Because of my house, which remains a ruin, while each of you is busy with your own house." (Haggai 1:9 NIV)

Examining our schedules for the times when we watch television, hang out on our phones, and so forth will help us replace this unproductive time with a Daily Retreat, even in the busyness of life. Even when we are truly too busy, God will help His intimate ones find a way. Thus, we grow in the desire to give God our best time. As our bonus, He makes sure that all of our important activities are completed.

You must present as the Lord's portion the best and holiest part of everything given to you [even your time]. (Numbers 18:29 NIV)

So do not fear, for I am with you; do not be dismayed, for I am your God. I will strengthen you and help you; I will uphold you with my righteous right hand. (Isaiah 41:10 NIV)

I HAVE NO TIME LEFT FOR YOU, JESUS

Back in the 1960s, a band called the Guess Who cut a song that perfectly depicts a life that is too busy for Jesus. The lyrics were quite simple, really. "I got no time, got no time, got no time. I got, got, got no time."

Pretty convicting, isn't it? Again, you and I receive some disciplined kicks in the rear from our wakeful Holy Spirit, who uses this type of hard knock to rouse us to our senses. Is it true that we have no time for Jesus, or does our adversary, the devil, just want us to believe it?

In my own life, to combat my lack of time in busy seasons, I simply get up thirty to sixty minutes earlier. For most of my life, I have awakened at 5:30 a.m. for my Daily Retreat time. When I changed jobs, however, and had to leave earlier, 5:30 changed to 5:00 a.m. Now, during this book-writing season, 5:00 has even changed to 4:00 a.m. (Jesus has never asked me to wake earlier than 4:00 a.m., but in my own mind, I like to think that 4:00 a.m. was the time Jesus awakened when He was on earth. That thought makes it easier for me to arise at that time.)

If I don't like how sleepy I feel, I just go to bed a bit earlier too. This has caused me to have to cut out the 10:00 p.m. news. No matter! There is 9:00 p.m. news in television land too.

Please don't think I am asking you to get up at 4:00 a.m. I am simply asking you to make time for Jesus in whatever way He speaks to you about it. And He will let you know. He is quite the gentleman and will urge you to make certain small changes, prodding you along to success, as He has done for me for the past four decades.

Here is the best part: time with Jesus is so rewarding. Whenever my alarm goes off, and I decide to get up fifteen minutes later, when I'm finished with my time with Jesus, I always wish I had just fifteen minutes more. You will be more than thankful that you made the necessary sacrifices to make time for Jesus.

I have vowed to never be too busy for my number one. I will go to great extremes to make time with Jesus as the very first engagement of my day. I pray and hope that you, too, will consider our Lord Jesus as more important than yourself because He is within you. He is entwining His ways into yours in an intricately unique and exquisite pattern. As it says in Song of Solomon 6:3a,

> I am my Beloved's and my Beloved is mine! (NIV)

ROADBLOCK FOUR: THE BELIEF THAT WE DO NOT REALLY NEED A DAILY RETREAT

When things are going well, we mistakenly believe we don't need a time for self-examination. Hey, all is rosy so what's the big deal? Why should I be required to practice Daily Retreat when life is practically perfect on Route 66 where (according to a song popularized by Nat King Cole, the Rolling Stones, and the Disney movie *Cars*) I'm getting my kicks? Our Holy Bible has a word or two to say about this:

> In his pride the wicked man does not seek him; in all his thoughts there is no room for God. (Psalm 10:4 NIV)

> The pride of your heart has deceived you, you who live in the clefts of the rocks and make your home on the heights, you who say to yourself, "Who can bring me down to the ground?" (Obadiah 1:3 NIV)

Such thinking hampers the relationship we previously developed with the Lord. Consistent time with Him keeps us in a right relationship.

> My eyes will be on the faithful in the land, that they may dwell with Me; the one whose walk is blameless will minister to Me. (Psalm 101:6 NIV)

RECOGNIZING SIN AND THE ONE WHO
KEEPS ME FROM IT; OR THE LEASH

One of the happiest moments of the day, according to my three-legged dog, MacGyver, is the second I pull out the leash from the shoe bin by the front door. Leaping and bounding, he prances around my feet encouraging me to *hurry up and put it on*, since that means we will be heading out on another great adventure (our usual one-mile route).

Because we travel this route daily together, more than once a curious thought has crossed my mind: *If I were to take MacGyver off his leash, I am positive he would follow me.* One day, with home in sight, I was ready to test my theory.

Just at that moment and without warning, a careless driver sped around the corner turning widely in our path. With all my strength, I yanked the leash—and the attached dog—to the safety of my neighbor's yard.

I shuddered to think what would have happened to MacGyver if I'd removed the leash. I realized that it was not only for his disobedience but more importantly for his protection that we were tied together.

The leash became a symbol to me of my relationship with God. As we walk in sync daily, the leash hangs loosely, and I am free to experience the adventure before me. When I stray off the path that God intends for me, however, I feel an unpleasant tug—my warning that all is not well, and I must pay closer attention to the sin in front of me—be it my own or the careless sin of someone careening down the road ahead.

May you and I visualize that when we are leashed to our Father in heaven, He steers us in the way we should go, not just once a week or once a month, but every day, both in fancy-free and nerve-racking times, with purpose and direction.

ROADBLOCK FIVE: UNWILLINGNESS TO FACE
GOD'S TRUTH OR GUIDANCE FOR US

It is our natural tendency to stay within our comfort zones, even if our behavior is sinful or undesirable. But God has other plans. He says, "There is a new and better way. Follow Me in it."

> See, I am doing a new thing! Now it springs up; do you not perceive
> it? I am making a way in the wilderness and streams in the wasteland.
> (Isaiah 43:19 NIV)

Perhaps we are comfortably in a rut, having lost our zest for life because we are afraid to go forward with God. God wants to lead us in a new direction.

> He tends his flock like a shepherd: He gathers the lambs in his arms and carries them close to his heart; he gently leads those that have young. (Isaiah 40:11 NIV)

There will be abundant rewards for the person who dares to trust his or her life to the one who has the greater perspective.

> He views the ends of the earth and sees everything under the heavens. (Job 28:24 NIV)

SEEING LIFE FROM GOD'S PERSPECTIVE: "WHAT YOU MEANT FOR HARM, GOD MEANT FOR GOOD"

Perspective. What's yours? What's mine? What is God's?

Here is the original version of a well-known perspective picture. Do you see a young beauty or an old hag?

MY WIFE AND MY MOTHER-IN-LAW
They are both in this picture — Find them

Or how about this drawing?

There are quite a few faulty perceptions. Do you see some of them? The man in the foreground is standing on thin air, if you view the so-called floor as a wall instead (note where the corners come together to see the wall as parallel to his shoes, except even the wall is inaccurate, as it does not come out to the ninety-degree angle in the corner, as it should).

Our earthly perspectives are not to be taken as total truth, as long as Jesus is working His will for us. This was Joseph's realization. In Genesis 50:20 (NIV), he reassured his brothers that he saw his life from God's perspective. Joseph understood that being abused, tormented, sold into slavery, and imprisoned unfairly was all for the ultimate good of his family and Israel as a nation. He could confidently say to them, "What you meant for harm, God meant for good."

An exquisite rose has no choice but to abide with the thorns that are a part of its design. Do the thorns take away from the rose's beauty, or do they make its elegance even more meaningful?

What does it take for you or me to change our fallible human viewpoint to God's preferable perspective? After all is said and done, the Master's mindset, regarding our lives and the circumstances that surround them, should be viewed as the best-designed plan of all when we willingly submit to His truth and guidance.

List some of your roadblocks.

1.

2.

3.

4.

5.

My Prayer: Dear Lord Jesus, I claim victory over these roadblocks and seek Your help and guidance to overcome them. Amen.

REST STOP: HOMEWORK TIME

It is homework time once again. The goal is to take five days out of the next seven to ten days to complete this assignment. There is no need to read farther along in this book at this time. Now, simply savor what we have gleaned thus far and practice scripture reflection with Jesus by your side on each of the homework days. Also, notice His presence with you if you skip a day in between, as He is still there, reminding you of what you and He learned together a day or two ago.

This homework is different on several accounts. First, the teachings are from Jesus's very heart and mouth. They are all "words in red" (in most Bibles, Jesus's words are shown in red ink), which makes it special to have Him speak directly to you and me, one-on-one.

A second difference is that you get to choose your own verse or set of verses from anything written in Matthew 5, 6, or 7. You may stay in Matthew 5 all week, or you may choose something in Matthew 7, then 5, then 6, back to 7, and finish with Matthew 6.

It doesn't matter. The goal here is to find a verse that pops out at you—choose the first one that does. When a verse pops out, it means the Holy Spirit would like you to consider it for your own life. Perhaps there is a change in this area that He wants you to implement. Perhaps you needed this encouragement because you have changed a negative attitude for a positive one.

The emphasis of Jesus's teachings is always on deep changes of heart and perspective. The words of our Lord and Savior are so profound that merely reading them is not enough. We must chew, as if we're eating a gooey caramel, on these new or even difficult teachings, reflecting on their exact, personal meaning for our inner mindset changes. How about these statements, found farther along in the Gospels of Matthew, Mark, Luke, and John:

> But many who are first will be last, and many who are last will be first. (Matthew 19:30 NIV)

> Whoever wants to become great among you must be your servant, and whoever wants to be first must be a slave of all. For even the Son of Man did not come to be served, but to serve, and to give his life as a ransom for many. (Mark 10:43–45 NASB)

> To everyone who has, more will be given, but as for the one who has nothing even what they have will be taken away. (Luke 19:26 NASB)

Anyone who loves their life will lose it, while anyone who hates their life in this world will keep it for eternal life. Whoever serves Me must follow Me; and where I am, my servant also will be. My Father will honor the one who serves Me. (John 12:25–26 NIV)

Hmmm. Am I first or last? Chew. Chew. How am I with serving? Chew. Chew. Am I given more, or is what I have taken away? Chew. Chew. Am I losing my life here for the sake of His kingdom there? Chew. Chew.

The enemies of Jesus hated such words. They considered them to be so offensive that the "chief priests and the teachers of the law heard this and began looking for a way to kill Him, for they feared Him, because the whole crowd was amazed at His teaching" (Mark 11:18 NIV).

How about you and me—do we disregard, take offense, or take the words of Jesus lightly? Or do we chew on them, asking for God's wisdom and guidance to direct our hearts and minds, as these words of life slowly but surely are ingested into our systems?

The Holy Spirit will use Jesus's direct teachings to convict, guide, admonish, and strengthen us. Let's allow Him the pleasure of having at us with gusto!

My prayer for you, right now, is that you will feel the love of Jesus this week as never before. I desire that Jesus will come alongside you wherever you are in your walk with Him and will that He wrap His arms of acceptance around you to give you excitement and peace. Amen, dear friend.

Happy homework days. See you soon.

CHAPTER 6 HOMEWORK DAY 1: SERMON ON THE MOUNT

Date:

Title: (insert at end of session)
Prayer: Speak personally to me, Lord Jesus.
Passage: Matthew 5, 6, or 7

Verse(s):

Personal Application:

Prayer:

Title: (reinsert at top of page)

Travel Journal Tip: The Importance of a Study Bible

OK, let's be honest. Some of what we read in the Bible is sort of confusing, isn't it? In days gone by, I recall reading the Beatitudes, the portion of scripture in Matthew 5:3–12, and wondering exactly what Jesus meant. For example, what did Jesus mean when He said, "Blessed are those who mourn, for they will be comforted" (Matthew 5:4 NIV)? In my twenties, I had not experienced much death. Hmmm. "Well, I guess I'll save that nugget for down the road a bit."

When I purchased my first study Bible, my comprehension increased. Regarding Matthew 5:4, my current study Bible says, *"those who mourn* Over both personal and corporate sins (see Ezra 9:4 and Psalm 119:36)."

Jesus was not only speaking about mourning over death, then, but also mourning over sin in general. That insight helped me to apply it, personally and currently. Let's look up those verses while we're at it. We see corporate sin in Ezra and personal sin in Psalm 119.

> Then everyone who trembled at the words of the God of Israel gathered around me because of this unfaithfulness of the exiles. And I sat there appalled until the evening sacrifice. (Ezra 9:4 NIV)

> Turn my heart toward your statutes and not toward selfish gain. (Psalm 119:36 NIV)

I no longer have to wonder what passages mean; I'm able to absorb more of Jesus's intent. With my study Bible I can glean greater significance for my life. My hope is that you, too, will have access to a study Bible for fuller perception and larger-scale growth.

Jesus is ready and willing to show you His meaning regarding scripture. Get with Him in prayer, and ask Him for His wisdom and discernment for any passage you do not understand.

CHAPTER 6 HOMEWORK DAY 2: SERMON ON THE MOUNT

Date:

Title: (insert at end of session)
Prayer: Lord Jesus, show me something I need to know.
Passage: Matthew 5, 6, or 7

Verse(s):

Personal Application:

Prayer:

Title: (reinsert at top of page)

THE CLASSICS

Who doesn't love and identify with a classic? Here are a few:

Classic author: Mark Twain   Classic candy: Hershey bar
Classic playwright: Shakespeare   Classic movie: *Home Alone*
Classic artist: Leonardo DaVinci   Classic car: Ford Mustang
Classic cartoon character: Mickey Mouse   Classic rock band: The Beatles
Classic dessert: apple pie and vanilla ice cream   Classic fast food: McDonald's

And who can argue about this choice?
Classic teacher: Jesus
Classic truths:

Do not store up for yourselves treasures on earth, where moths and vermin destroy, and where thieves break in and steal. But store up for yourselves treasures in heaven, where moths and vermin do not destroy, and where thieves do not break in and steal. For where your treasure is, there your heart will be also. (Matthew 6:19–21 NIV)

Therefore everyone who hears these words of Mine and puts them into practice is like a wise man who built his house on the rock. The rain came down, the streams rose, and the winds blew and beat against that house; yet it did not fall, because it had its foundation on the rock. But everyone who hears these words of Mine and does not put them into practice is like a foolish man who built his house on sand. The rain came down, the streams rose, and the winds blew and beat against that house, and it fell with a great crash. (Matthew 7:24–27 NIV)

What a pleasure for you and me to sit daily at the feet of our master teacher, Jesus, and learn His classic truths, which will never lose value.

CHAPTER 6 HOMEWORK DAY 3: SERMON ON THE MOUNT

Date:

Title: (insert at end of session)
Prayer: Lord Jesus, You have the words of life because You are the Word (John 1:14).
Passage: Matthew 5, 6, or 7

Verse(s):

Personal Application:

Prayer:

Title: (reinsert at top of page)

"Pray Like This!"

In Matthew 6:5–13 (NIV), Jesus says, "And when you pray …"

Don't

1. be like the hypocrites who pray to be seen by others (Matthew 6:5).
2. keep babbling with many words because God knows what you need (Matthew 6:7).

Do

1. Go into your room, close the door, and pray to Father God. Then your Father, who sees what is done in secret, will reward you (Matthew 6:6).
2. Pray like this: our Father in heaven, holy is Your name (Matthew 6:9).
3. Your kingdom come, Your will be done on earth as it is also done in heaven (Matthew 6:10).
4. Give us this day our daily bread (Matthew 6:11).
5. Forgive us our debts as we also forgive our debtors (Matthew 6:12).
6. Lead us not into temptation, but deliver us from the evil one (Matthew 6:13).

In prayer, Jesus wants you to get with Him in secret and

- acknowledge God's holiness;
- seek God's will to be done through you as His follower or by other means;
- ask for your daily needs to be met;
- confess your sin, receive forgiveness, and do the same for others who sin against you; and
- be led by Father God in the way of righteousness, thus refuting temptation and sending Satan packing!

Prayer

Thank you, Jesus, for showing us how You want us to pray.

Father God, You are holy. Here I am, Your humble servant. May Your will be done in this world, using me however You see fit to help You get it done. Please meet my needs along with my family's needs. I ask forgiveness for my sins today. So, too, give me Your grace to forgive those who sin against me. Let me not succumb to temptation, but lead me on Your righteous path today. I ask most humbly. Amen!

CHAPTER 6 HOMEWORK DAY 4: SERMON ON THE MOUNT

Date:

Title: (insert at end of session)
Prayer: Here I am. Change me, Jesus.
Passage: Matthew 5, 6, or 7

Verse(s):

Personal Application:

Prayer:

Title: (reinsert at top of page)

Persistent Prayer = Good Gifts from God

Jesus loved to teach about persistence in the hearts of His followers. Read about such an instance in Luke18:1–8 (MSG):

> Jesus told them a story showing that it was necessary for them to pray consistently and never quit. He said, "There was once a judge in some city who never gave God a thought and cared nothing for people. A widow in that city kept after him: 'My rights are being violated. Protect me!'
>
> "He never gave her the time of day. But after this went on and on, he said to himself, 'I care nothing what God thinks, even less what people think. But because this widow won't quit badgering me, I'd better do something and see that she gets justice—otherwise I'm going to end up beaten black-and-blue by her pounding.'"
>
> Then the Master said, "Do you hear what that judge, corrupt as he is, is saying? So what makes you think God won't step in and work justice for his chosen people, who continue to cry out for help? Won't he stick up for them? I assure you, he will. He will not drag his feet."

One of the sets of verses that popped out at me this week was Matthew 7:7–11:

> Ask and it will be given to you; seek and you will find; knock and the door will be opened to you. For everyone who asks receives; the one who seeks finds; and to the one who knocks, the door will be opened. "Which of you, if your son asks for bread, will give him a stone? Or if he asks for a fish, will give him a snake? If you, then, though you are evil, know how to give good gifts to your children, how much more will your Father in heaven give good gifts to those who ask him!

What good gifts have you been given due to your persistent prayers? Here are a few of mine:

- Travel mercies for my husband in his weekly travels
- Financial needs always met
- Calm, peace, and faith in God in this life of constant stress or concern
- My children blessed with wonderful spouses
- God's protection over my children and grandchildren

What good gifts have you asked for that you have not yet seen? How about these:

- Health for ourselves, family members, and/or friends
- A change in circumstances for difficulties
- For today, a change in attitude for difficulties
- Eyes to see and ears to hear, for us or for others

Persistent prayer is both a privilege we can implement, per Jesus, and the means of receiving an answer. Amen!

CHAPTER 6 HOMEWORK DAY 5: SERMON ON THE MOUNT

Date:

Title: (insert at end of session)
Prayer: Lord Jesus, give me Your wisdom for today.
Passage: Matthew 5, 6, or 7

Verse(s):

Personal Application:

Prayer:

Title: (reinsert at top of page)

GOD'S GOOD GIFTS, OR CHOCOLATE SYRUP

As I was reading Matthew 6:25–26, 33 (NIV), I couldn't help but remember two days in my life and in the life of my fifth child, Tom, when we saw these verses fulfilled.

> Therefore, I tell you, do not worry about your life, what you will eat or drink; or about your body, what you will wear. Is not life more than food, and the body more than clothes? Look at the birds of the air; they do not sow or reap or store away in barns, and yet your heavenly Father feeds them. Are you not much more valuable than they? … But seek first his kingdom and his righteousness, and all these things will be given to you as well.

It was early June 2002, during Vacation Bible School week. My four younger children were all involved, and I was the preschool Bible teacher. On the way home from church that Tuesday afternoon, we stopped in at the grocery store to pick up a few items.

As we walked the aisles together, Tom, age six, saw a large bottle of chocolate syrup on the shelf and asked me if we could get it. We were living on a budget, and I knew that I had to make careful choices to feed a family of eight. "Tom, I'm so sorry," I said. "We can't get chocolate syrup today, but we can get milk." Thus, we toted several gallons in hand to last us through the week.

The next morning, Wednesday, was the day I was to teach the salvation message to the youngest children. While reviewing this lesson in the story circle on the floor before the children arrived, a woman from the Outreach Team came into the classroom with a large box of food and canned goods for my family.

"I have eight children, and I know how tough it can be," she said, placing the box on the floor in front me.

On top of the generous mound of pasta, spaghetti sauce, and cereal was a large bottle of chocolate syrup, exactly like the one Tom had asked me to buy the day before. I screamed, *"Chocolate syrup!"*

Her quick response was, "Oh no, does your family have chocolate allergies?"

With tears in my eyes, I told her the meaning behind this God gift that was personalized for Tom.

I used this divine lesson of God's love and provision for His beloved little precious ones with the children that day. And you can bet the Oury family had a prayer of thanksgiving plus delicious chocolate milk on our lips that evening for dinner!

DAILY RETREAT EVALUATION

1. **What worked for you?**

2. **What did not work for you? What was difficult? What needs to change?**

3. **Pray over the difficulties with God.**

4. **What did you learn? How did the Lord speak to you or use you?**

5. **What excites you? What are your hopes?**

PART 3

GAINING MOMENTUM

Leo climbs a ladder on a trail in Acadia National Park, Bar Harbor, Maine

7

AREAS OF PERSONAL GROWTH

JESUS'S DEEP LOVE AND NEED FOR YOU

I hope you are finding moments to spend with Jesus, sitting at His feet, working on your master's program with Him. What have you learned thus far from Him?

We have reached an exciting turning point in this book. Up until now, we have gone through the basics and then focused on how to actualize this practice of spending time with Jesus. You may have steered through some rough terrain in the process. I hope you have figured out what is and is not working for your particular circumstance. If you still struggle, please look for helpful suggestions online via the link found in the "How to Use This Book" section.

For the next four chapters, our focus shifts to all the benefits of practicing a Daily Retreat. Primarily, you are to know and understand how deep, how wide, and how high the Father's love is for you. Ephesians 3:17b–19 (NIV) says this perfectly:

> And I pray that you, being rooted and established in love, may have power, together with all the Lord's holy people, to grasp how wide and long and high and deep is the love of Christ, and to know this love that surpasses knowledge—that you may be filled to the measure of all the fullness of God.

Next, He is thrilled to invite you to partner with Him in showing people who Jesus is by just being you in your sphere of influence. You are chosen and appointed to be His ambassador, just as 2 Corinthians 5:20 (NIV) says,

> We are therefore Christ's ambassadors, as though God were making his appeal through us. We implore you on Christ's behalf: Be reconciled to God.

Life cannot be more fulfilling than when these two concepts are merged. Throughout the remaining chapters, we will strive to bring God's love and need for you and me to the forefront of our minds. I hope you are getting excited to think of yourself as a crucial player in God's kingdom on earth. He has exciting assignments for you to complete, which will allow the gospel to be spread. Daily Retreat is a key way that it happens.

SEVEN AREAS OF PERSONAL GROWTH

The Lord Jesus would like that you and I grasp an overall understanding of the unique life He has given each of us. In this chapter, you will gain a perspective on your life—from a microscopic view to a telescopic vista. As I have progressed in my relationship with Jesus, He has shown me seven areas of my life in which He works to change me, show me, use me, and send me, from the inner soul to the realms of eternity. These seven areas are:

1. Purifying your inner being
2. Refining your close relationships
3. Affecting your sphere of influence
4. Deepening your love for the Trinity (Father, Son, and Holy Spirit) and deepening your prayer life
5. Impacting the world
6. Identifying with suffering and hardship
7. Envisioning eternity

Let's gain a better understanding of each of these areas of our lives.

AREA ONE: PURIFYING YOUR INNER BEING

The Lord will begin by conforming your attitudes and thoughts to His. Character qualities such as thankfulness, humility, and genuineness will become yours. He will give you daily assignments, such as, "Replace anger with patience," or "Do not make promises you cannot keep, and keep the promises you make," or "Cast your anxiety upon Me, and I will give you peace in spite of your circumstances." The purification and refining process of our inner beings ends when we step through the gates of heaven. Jesus spoke of this purification process when He said, "Blessed are the pure in heart, for they shall see God" (Matthew 5:8 NASB).

The apostle Paul, in his writing to the Corinthians, spoke of the inner transformation of our thoughts.

> We take captive every thought to make it obedient to Christ. (2 Corinthians 10:5b NIV)

We are witness to such inner change, not due to our own work but because we have allowed the Holy Spirit to take control through our availability and humility. It's an incredible change for the better!

THE MIRACULOUS TRANSFORMING OF A MINDSET

The scripture is full of treasure for us. Have you unearthed a diamond, ruby, or emerald? Have you gained gold or silver or pewter, which will withstand the fire of worldly trials? These treasures are verses of truth that transform an incomplete human mind into the beautiful mind of Christ.

I recently found treasure in the book of Philippians, which came down to this: the transforming of our minds—to believe and know the truth of Jesus Christ—is of the utmost importance. In Philippians, Paul, who at this time was known to all as Saul, says that he was living the dream of an upwardly mobile Jew; plus, he was zealous about doing the right thing, which was persecuting Christians. There was no doubt in his mind that he was correct and was on the right path to obtaining his own righteousness.

Yet Jesus Himself stopped Saul dead in his tracks while he was on the road to Damascus (Acts 9), surprising him with blindness to get his attention, letting Saul know that he had a wrong perception of truth, and showing him how he was living out of God's will. From that moment on, Paul (thus renamed by Jesus) was transformed by the renewing of his mind (Romans 12:2) and sought to be taught of Jesus in this new way of thinking. He renounced his old way of thinking and said,

> But whatever things were gain to me [the good life] those things I have counted as loss for the sake of Christ. More than that, I count all things to be loss in view of the surpassing value of knowing Christ Jesus my Lord, for whom I have suffered the loss of all things [especially his old way of thinking] and count them as rubbish in order that I may gain Christ, and may be found in Him, not having a righteousness of my own derived from the Law, but that which is through faith in Christ, the righteousness which comes from God on the basis of faith … I do not regard myself as having laid hold of it yet, but one thing I do: forgetting what lies behind and reaching forward to what lies ahead, I press on toward the goal for the prize of the upward call of God in Christ Jesus. (Philippians 3:7–9, 13–14 NASB)

My call and plea for my own life and for yours is that we allow Jesus to transform our thinking into His truth. As Paul said, we have to press on to this goal ourselves, pursuing it with all of our hearts. These are the truths on which we are supposed to dwell:

> Finally, brethren, whatever is true, whatever is honorable, whatever is right, whatever is pure, whatever is lovely, whatever is of good repute, if there is any excellence and if anything worthy of praise, let your mind dwell on these things. (Philippians 4:8 NASB)

We must believe the truth of scripture—that God values us beyond our comprehension and will stop at nothing to get our attention to that fact, as He did for Paul. He has a purpose for each one of us and will arrange our circumstances so that His purpose may be accomplished. He has set us securely on high and will guide us in paths of righteousness. Even if we pass through the shadowy darkness, He is with us.

These are mind-altering truths that can be ours if we take time to let Jesus teach us. Our old ways do not die without a fight—they resist—but Jesus is the victor when we allow Him control, and we listen to and obey His promptings. Slowly but surely, day by day, verse by verse, our minds begin to transform and we "have this attitude in ourselves which was also in Christ Jesus" (Philippians 2:5 NASB).

These crucial inner changes bring about all the remaining outer changes.

AREA TWO: REFINING YOUR CLOSE RELATIONSHIPS

The Lord is in the business of restoring relationships. He longs for us to live in harmony with our spouses, children, parents, extended families, and brothers and sisters in Christ. Here are some scriptures to prove it:

Husbands and Wives

Submit to one another out of reverence for Christ. Wives, submit yourselves to your own husbands as you do to the Lord ... Husbands, love your wives, just as Christ loved the church and gave himself up for her ... In this same way, husbands ought to love their wives as their own bodies. He who loves his wife loves himself." (Ephesians 5:21–22, 25, 28 NIV)

Children to Parents

Children, obey your parents in the Lord, for this is right. "Honor your father and mother"—which is the first commandment with a promise— "so that it may go well with you and that you may enjoy long life on the earth." Ephesians 6:1–3 NIV

Fathers (and Mothers Too) to Children

Fathers, do not exasperate your children; instead, bring them up in the training and instruction of the Lord. (Ephesians 6:4 NIV)

People to People

Therefore, if you are offering your gift at the altar and there remember that your brother or sister has something against you, leave your gift there in front of the altar. First go and be reconciled to them; then come and offer your gift. (Matthew 5:23–24 NIV)

Based on the idea of relationship restoration, Jesus will give you assignments such as, "Do not try to change your spouse. Watch the relationship change by your own submission and love," or "Speak words of love and encouragement to your children daily," or "Be first to apologize and seek forgiveness in any broken relationship." Not all relationships will be restored immediately, and perhaps some relationships will never be fully restored, but the Lord Jesus desires that your own work be complete in it through His help. He will guide you in the way you should go.

ENJOYING "RELATIONAL ROSES," EVEN WHEN CIRCUMSTANCES ARE THORNY

In 2010, my husband, Leo, had been unemployed for nearly two years due to the economic crisis of 2008. Our hearts were unified in daily prayer for God to "get us out of this mess—and now!" But that year, as I read Jeremiah 29, a new truth about the terrible trial of unemployment struck me like a bolt of lightning. God had told the Israelites ahead of time that they would be captive in Babylon for seventy years, yet they were not to sit around and cry about it. Instead, they were instructed to thrive, despite their undesirable surroundings.

> This is what the Lord Almighty, the God of Israel, says to all those I carried into exile from Jerusalem to Babylon: "Build houses and settle down; plant gardens and eat what they produce. Marry and have sons and daughters; find wives for your sons and give your daughters in marriage, so that they too may have sons and daughters. Increase in number there; do not decrease … When seventy years are completed for Babylon, I will come to you and fulfill my good promise to bring you back to this place. For I know the plans I have for you," declares the Lord, "plans to prosper you and not to harm you, plans to give you hope and a future." (Jeremiah 29:4–6, 12–13 NIV)

As I applied these verses to my own life, I entertained a thought: *What if unemployment lasts another sixty-eight years?* We decided then and there that God already knew the deep cries of our hearts to be released from this trial. Instead, we began to pray for eyes to see the opportunities to thrive under these adverse conditions.

One immediate revelation was that our three youngest children, who were still at home and in their mid-teen, early teen, and preteen phases, had daily quality time with their dad. Leo, who had traveled for a living, was now home to attend every football and softball game, wrestling match, special event, and award ceremony. Leo also spoke with them regularly about current events and how to see these events with a biblical worldview. The time to linger and love on our growing teens was a precious gift. Ironically, we began to see that the thorn of unemployment brought relational roses instead.

In what area of life are you crying out for release? Where might you nurture relational roses with your special family members in this tenacious trial? God hears and knows. He desires that we live each day fully and faithfully, content and purposeful to thrive in our relationships in any challenging situation that comes our way. He has plans to prosper us and to give us a future full of hope, while we make the best of difficult times with loved ones by our sides.

AREA THREE: AFFECTING YOUR SPHERE OF INFLUENCE

Your church, neighborhood, community, and workplace will be better because you are using your time, talents, and treasures to serve the Lord in these places. The following verses confirm the importance of your place in the world right around you:

> Your love has given me great joy and encouragement, because you, believer, have refreshed the hearts of the Lord's people. (Philemon 1:7 NIV)

> For the entire law is fulfilled in keeping this one command: "Love your neighbor as yourself." (Galatians 5:14 NIV)

The Lord Jesus will give you assignments such as, "Sign up to be an usher at church, and put your own tithe in the offering plate each week too," or "Introduce yourself to your new neighbors, and take a take a plate of cookies to them," or "Take a bag of clothes to the rescue mission and volunteer," or "Invite your coworker to Thanksgiving dinner." Your notepad is a good place to jot down the marching orders you receive in the midst of having your Daily Retreat time. These special undertakings become your to-do list.

ASSUMPTIONS, ACCUSATIONS, AND ADVICE

One of the major issues in the book of Job (pronounced *Jobe*) is how to be a good counselor and friend to those in our spheres of influence. Job's "friends" made many negative assumptions and accusations, along with giving hurtful advice. What is a fair response from us when someone is battered and bruised in the hardships of life?

Because I am a hospice worker, I attended a seminar for people who experience second-hand trauma in their employment. There also were nurses, victim's advocates, counselors, emergency dispatchers, and first responders there—those who see the worst-case scenarios every day. One phrase that most impacted me when answering someone's questions regarding difficult circumstances was this: "It's hard to know."

It *is* hard to know why someone experiences trauma. I added a second phrase: *It's hard to know, but God knows.*

In our own difficulties of life, a good, nonjudgmental friend is a true gift. Pouring our hearts out to a listening ear is healthfully beneficial to the process of restoration. Even Jesus Himself qualifies as that listening ear, as He says,

> Take my yoke upon you and learn from me, for I am gentle and humble in heart, and you will find rest for your souls. (Matthew 11:29 NIV)

As Christian friends, let us steer clear of making assumptions and accusations. Our own listening ears or a nod of the head is a perfect gesture to indicate our love and support for a devastated soul. Let's allow carefully chosen words to proceed from our lips to promote healing.

> Let your conversation be always full of grace, seasoned with salt, so that you may know how to answer everyone. (Colossians 4:6 NIV)

May we seek to be helpful friends who give wise counsel when someone in our sphere of influence experiences trauma.

AREA FOUR: DEEPENING YOUR LOVE FOR THE TRINITY (FATHER, SON, AND HOLY SPIRIT) AND DEEPENING YOUR PRAYER LIFE

You will see God's deep love for you as your prayers are answered, as you see His hand on situations, and as you experience His presence in your own life.

> For the Lord will go before you, the God of Israel will be your rear guard. (Isaiah 52:12b NIV)

Jesus's active involvement in your life will bring you assurance, comfort, and peace in chaotic times.

> Peace I leave with you; my peace I give you. I do not give to you as the world gives. Do not let your hearts be troubled and do not be afraid. (John 14:27 NIV)

The Holy Spirit will embolden you and push you to new places you would have never gone before.

> But you will receive power when the Holy Spirit comes on you; and you will be my witnesses in Jerusalem, and in all Judea and Samaria, and to the ends of the earth. (Acts 1:8 NIV)

Worship and praise will become more meaningful to you.

> I bowed down and worshiped the Lord. I praised the Lord, the God of my master Abraham, who had led me on the right road. (Genesis 24:48 NIV)

You will seek Jesus and converse with Him throughout the day in prayer. You will be honored to pray with and for others.

> Therefore confess your sins to each other and pray for each other so that you may be healed. The prayer of a righteous person is powerful and effective. (James 5:16 NIV)

You will share in the hurts of others by giving to them in sacrificial ways. Jesus will give you assignments such as, "Give a gift card to a family who is unemployed at Christmas," or "Sit with someone at the hospital while his [or her] loved one is having surgery," or "Pray for and support a widow financially for a year after the death of her husband."

> Carry each other's burdens, and in this way, you will fulfill the law of Christ. (Galatians 6:2 NIV)

You will be blessed to be a blessing to those who are hurting because of your own deeper connection to the Savior.

INVASION OF THE MIND AND BODY SNATCHER: THE STRATEGIC TAKEOVER OF THE HOLY SPIRIT

Did you know that according to 1 Corinthians 6:19 (NASB), "You are not your own"?

While many a spooky story has been written with this idea in mind, for those who are in Christ Jesus, this is very excellent news! Each and every one of us who has surrendered our lives to the Lord Jesus Christ has had this "invasion" occur. The

Holy Spirit, with all authority, sets up His command post in our hearts and begins His strategic takeover. Slowly but surely, what was once pleasing to us in life BC (before Christ), now becomes more and more distasteful in life AD (after deployment)!

Just as pure water is tainted by only a speck of dirt, so our hearts—abodes of the Holy Spirit—are tainted by even the subtlest of sins. The Holy Spirit daily maneuvers the merger of His mind with ours, thwarting Satan's tactics by eliminating his imprint on our lives.

Our quest is to reject and eject any and all impurity. As we willingly collaborate, the Holy Spirit's peaceful presence rules, and the Lord's reign in your heart and mine is accomplished. May we cooperate in the conquest because we are not our own!

Enjoy these verses regarding the Holy Spirit's takeover:

> Do you not know that your bodies are temples of the Holy Spirit, who is in you, whom you have received from God? You are not your own. (1 Corinthians 6:19 NASB)

> But the Advocate, the Holy Spirit, whom the Father will send in My name, will teach you all things and will remind you of everything I have said to you. (John 14:26 NIV)

WHICH CAME FIRST—THE VICTORY OR THE PRAYER?

When reading about the life of David, who was a mighty warrior for God, we find that David commemorated many of his experiences, both in battle and in life, in the psalms. Psalm 20 is a prayer David wrote in regard to a battle he fought, which was recorded in 2 Samuel 10. After reading these two chapters together, it struck me that David must have written Psalm 20 after he had victory in the battle he'd faced because Psalm 20 matched so perfectly.

But then I thought, *No, David would have been praying for God's protection for his warriors beforehand.* Therefore, Psalm 20 is David's prayer for his men before they went into battle and his encouragement to them to believe that God would indeed answer, via their future victory:

> May the Lord answer you when you are in distress;
> may the name of the God of Jacob protect you.
> May he send you help from the sanctuary
> and grant you support from Zion.

May he remember all your sacrifices
and accept your burnt offerings.
May he give you the desire of your heart
and make all your plans succeed.
May we shout for joy over your victory
and lift up our banners in the name of our God.
May the Lord grant all your requests …
Some trust in chariots and some in horses,
but we trust in the name of the Lord our God.
They are brought to their knees and fall,
but we rise up and stand firm.
Lord, give victory to the king!
Answer us when we call!

After reading this, I began my own list of answered prayers; I could have gone on and on. Think back over your life. There are answered prayers for every day you and I have lived, even answers for which we never prayed.

Make a list of ten answers to prayer. Like me, you could continue on to one hundred with more time and contemplation:

1.   6.
2.   7.
3.   8.
4.   9.
5.   10.

Incredible, isn't it? What prayer requests are before Yahweh's bowl of incense right now? Is there any reason to believe that they will go unheard? Prepare for answered prayer in His way and in His time. Amen.

Reflect on the following verses regarding prayer and answered prayer:

And when he had taken it, the four living creatures and the twenty-four elders fell down before the Lamb. Each one had a harp, and they were holding golden bowls full of incense, which are the prayers of God's people. (Revelation 5:8 NIV)

He answered their prayers, because they trusted in Him. (1 Chronicles 5:20b NIV)

AREA FIVE: IMPACTING THE WORLD

As you develop this close connection to Jesus, your heart will begin to lean toward certain areas of service. You will develop passions based on your God-given talents and God-directed desires. You will gain understanding for how best to ultimately serve the Lord. Jesus will give you assignments such as, "Serve for a week on a missions trip," or "Begin a prayer group or Bible study with some like-minded women or men," or "Use your artistic talents to _____," or "Start a support group for those experiencing _____."

Your own personally unique spiritual gifts, plus life experiences, will be used by God in a refreshing way to glorify Him and bless the world around you. Ask God to help you discern His call for your life. Reflect on the following verses, which speak to the call of God on your life.

> Each person should live as a believer in whatever situation the Lord has assigned to them, just as God has called them. (1 Corinthians 7:17 NIV)

> As a prisoner for the Lord, I, Paul, urge you to live a life worthy of the calling you have received. (Ephesians 4:1 NIV)

TAKE THE LAND! STEPS TO MOVING FORWARD WITH GOD

Reading the end of Deuteronomy is like reading the last page of a good book. Throughout the book, Moses reviews the entire history of the forty years of wandering in the desert and says his own farewells to the Israelites before passing away to eternity. I desired to sit in reflection and wonder at this unprecedented experience.

God, however, does not share my sense of sentimentality. He has work to do! In fact, the beginning of Joshua, just one page later, is quite abrupt, for God told Joshua, "Moses my servant is dead. Now then, you and all these people, get ready to cross the Jordan River into the land I am about to give you" (Joshua 1:2 NIV). Wow! See ya later, Moses. Joshua's on the move!

I realized that God is all about advancing His purposes. He will not rest or kick back until His work is accomplished. Moses had served His purposes in an unparalleled way, but time was marching forward, and Joshua was now God's earthly focus.

God gave Joshua a motivational pep talk as he was prepped to conquer the promised land:

⁷ "Be strong and very courageous. Be careful to obey all the law my servant Moses gave you; do not turn from it to the right or to the left, that you may be successful wherever you go. ⁸ Keep this Book of the Law always on your lips; meditate on it day and night, so that you may be careful to do everything written in it. Then you will be prosperous and successful. ⁹ Have I not commanded you? Be strong and courageous. Do not be afraid; do not be discouraged, for the Lord your God will be with you wherever you go … ¹¹ Now, go through the camp and tell the people, 'Get your provisions ready. Three days from now you will cross the Jordan here to go in and take possession of the land the Lord your God is giving you for your own.'" (Joshua 1:7–9, 11 NIV)

What are the steps you and I may incorporate as we, too, move forward spiritually, emotionally, or physically into new assignments from God?

1. **Show strength** (Joshua 1:7). Moving forward is not for wimps. It takes a strong resolve to say goodbye to the past and hello to a new normal.
2. **Be courageous** (verse 7). There will be circumstances and people who discourage us from a new normal, since living where we are right now is so much easier and way more comfortable. Courageously, we must stand against these temptations to stay in the realm of the familiar.
3. **Stay on course** (verse 7). In new territory, you and I can get waylaid by the surroundings. We can hold back, regress, or veer off the path. Following God on the path of forward progress is the sure route to success.
4. **Know and speak God's Word** (verse 8). Our study and knowledge of God and His Word is important and not in vain. His truth has the power that you and I need to continue.
5. **Reflect on God's Word daily** (verse 8). This habit centers us day to day so that we may remember the goal of "forward progress with God," which is always before us.
6. **Replace negative thoughts with faith** (verse 9). As we travel uncharted territory, fear and discouragement can be overwhelming. This is exactly the point where faith—a positive reaction to negative circumstances—takes over. Faith knows "if God is for us, who can be against us?" (Romans 8:31b NIV).
7. **Claim God's presence every moment** (verse 9). There is no greater resolve for our lives than to repeat God's own words to ourselves—"The Lord my God will be with me wherever I go" (Joshua 1:9 NIV).

8. **Expect to conquer the land** (verse 11)! Step out in faith into your new assignment victoriously and be amazed at what God will accomplish through you.

Which "land" shall you and I conquer with God's help? Have we received and believed our pep talk from God? He will see us through to victory as we incorporate His truths into our lives.

AREA SIX: IDENTIFYING WITH SUFFERING AND HARDSHIP

You will understand suffering—such as health problems; unemployment or low income; loss through natural disaster; divorce; tragic situations; abuse, neglect, or persecution; separation from or the death of loved ones—more personally, either through your own hardship or the difficulties of people close to you. It is in this place of suffering and hardship where absolute faith is experienced firsthand, as only Jesus Christ Himself comprehends your situation completely. As you experience devastation due to living in a world of sin, you will turn to Christ, who alone can save, comfort, heal, and uphold you in your time of darkness. He will give you assignments such as, "Cry out to Me moment by moment, and I will bring relief," or "Be assured that I still love you and know your needs."

Reflect on the following scripture encouragements for times when suffering is a part of your life:

> Praise be to the God and Father of our Lord Jesus Christ, the Father of compassion and the God of all comfort, who comforts us in all our troubles, so that we can comfort those in any trouble with the comfort we ourselves receive from God. For just as we share abundantly in the sufferings of Christ, so also our comfort abounds through Christ. (2 Corinthians 1:3–5 NIV)

> Blessed is the one who perseveres under trial because, having stood the test, that person will receive the crown of life that the Lord has promised to those who love him. (James 1:12 NIV)

PROCLAMATIONS OF FAITH AMID SUFFERING

The book of Job, found in the Old Testament, speaks to the issue of hardship and suffering. Job, a God-fearing man, had so much about which to complain, and he openly voiced those sentiments to God in his humanity. Yet in the thick of such severe suffering, he also voiced some of the most beloved words found in the Bible, attesting simultaneously to his continued, unwavering faith in God.

> Though He slay me, yet will I hope in Him. (Job 13:15 NIV)

> Even now my Witness is in heaven; my Advocate is on high. My Intercessor is my Friend as my eyes pour out tears to God; on behalf of a man, He pleads with God as One pleads for a friend. (Job 16:19–21 NIV)

> I know that my Redeemer lives, and that in the end He will stand on the earth. And after my skin has been destroyed, yet in my flesh I will see God; I myself will see Him with my own eyes—I, and not another. How my heart yearns within me! (Job 19:25–27 NIV)

As you or I have reason to cry out to God and even lament our desperate conditions, may we also, like Job, voice words of faith concurrently.

The apostle Paul was another who suffered greatly for his faith while bound in prison and, just like Job, proclaimed his belief in God, who had it all in His control:

> So do not be ashamed of the testimony about our Lord or of me His prisoner. Rather, join with me in suffering for the gospel, by the power of God ... And of this gospel I was appointed a herald and an apostle and a teacher. That is why I am suffering as I am. Yet this is no cause for shame, because I know Whom I have believed, and am convinced that He is able to guard what I have entrusted to Him until that day. (2 Timothy 1:8, 11–12 NIV)

Like Job and Paul in their sufferings, may you and I release our own concerns and prayers to the throne room of heaven, while also proclaiming our faith in God, who knows our afflictions.

Area Seven: Envisioning Eternity

As you become more intimate with Jesus Christ, you will realize that this world is truly not your home, that you are a stranger and an alien here, and that the ultimate goal is to be with Jesus Christ in heaven. Fear of death is removed because the teachings of Jesus regarding our eternal home become second nature.

"Very truly I tell you, whoever hears my word and believes him who sent me has eternal life and will not be judged but has crossed over from death to life." (John 5:24 NIV)

"My Father's house has many rooms; if that were not so, would I have told you that I am going there to prepare a place for you? And if I go and prepare a place for you, I will come back and take you to be with me that you also may be where I am … I will not leave you as orphans; I will come to you. Before long, the world will not see me anymore, but you will see me. Because I live, you also will live." (John 14:2–3, 18–19 NIV)

Understanding that eternal life brings new and greater realities elicits excitement and hope for the wonder to come. Ingest this thought from Paul:

Some skeptic is sure to ask, "Show me how resurrection works. Give me a diagram; draw me a picture. What does this 'resurrection body' look like?" If you look at this question closely, you realize how absurd it is. There are no diagrams for this kind of thing. We do have a parallel experience in gardening. You plant a "dead" seed; soon there is a flourishing plant. There is no visual likeness between seed and plant. You could never guess what a tomato would look like by looking at a tomato seed. What we plant in the soil and what grows out of it don't look anything alike. The dead body that we bury in the ground and the resurrection body that comes from it will be dramatically different … The corpse that's planted is no beauty, but when it's raised, it's glorious. Put in the ground weak, it comes up powerful … but what a difference from when it goes down in physical mortality to when it is raised up in spiritual immortality! (1 Corinthians 15:35–38, 43–44 MSG)

As astonishing as this will be, you also understand that your purpose here on earth has not yet been completed, and you seek your next assignment as a son or daughter of the King of kings. Your assignment is the same as Queen Esther's, who heard, "And who knows whether you have attained your current status for such a time as this!" (Esther 4:14b NIV).

FROM MOURNING TO DANCING: EXPERIENCING RESURRECTION JOY NOW!

God is fully able to turn the tables of sadness into joy, mourning into dancing, and weeping into elation. As a beautiful example for you and me, David experienced great trouble; then God's work on his behalf, and finally there was a praiseworthy change of circumstances:

> I will exalt you, Lord, for you lifted me out of the depths and did not let my enemies gloat over me. Lord my God, I called to you for help, and you healed me … You turned my wailing into dancing; you removed my sackcloth and clothed me with joy, that my heart may sing your praises and not be silent. Lord my God, I will praise you forever. (Psalm 30:1–2, 11–12 NIV)

In John 20, this same resurrection joy was experienced by Mary Magdalene, who had also endured extreme mourning, God's power, and her own praiseworthy change of circumstances.

> Now Mary stood outside the tomb crying. As she wept, she bent over to look into the tomb and saw two angels in white, seated where Jesus' body had been, one at the head and the other at the foot. They asked her, "Woman, why are you crying?" She said, "They have taken my Lord away and I don't know where they have put him." At this, she turned around and saw Jesus standing there, but she did not realize that it was Jesus. He asked her, "Woman, why are you crying? Who is it you are looking for?" Thinking he was the gardener, she said, "Sir, if you have carried him away, tell me where you have put him, and I will get him." Jesus said to her, "Mary." She turned toward him and cried out in Aramaic, "Rabboni!" (which means "Teacher"). Jesus said, "Do not hold on to me, for I have not yet ascended to the Father. Go instead to my brothers and tell them, 'I am ascending to my Father and your Father, to my God and your God.'" Mary Magdalene went to the disciples with the news: "I have seen the Lord!" And she told them that he had said these things to her. (John 20:11–18 NIV)

I began to wonder if I, like Mary, also have failed to recognize the true change of circumstances that surround me, for Jesus was right there but remained unperceived.

What glory encompasses you or me, yet our spiritual sight is too dim to comprehend it? Lord Jesus, may we fathom the divine reality, not the earthly assumption.

God wants us to taste and see His goodness through our faith in Him, ahead of time, in belief of His authority. Our mourning will indeed be turned to dancing as we entrust Him with the hardships of life. Let us praise Jesus that resurrection joy may be ours today, knowing that He will turn death into life and dead ends into highways.

Together, Jesus and I came up with the following diagram depicting the areas of personal growth that you and I will experience, from inner soul to eternity, as we spend time with the Lord in Daily Retreat. On which area is Jesus focusing with you right now? Oftentimes, He works with us on several areas at once.

We will continuously grow in every area, with time and personal application of the scriptures that He uses to change our lives.

Areas of Personal Growth Diagram

List one hope you have for yourself in each of the seven areas of growth. The domains are as follows:

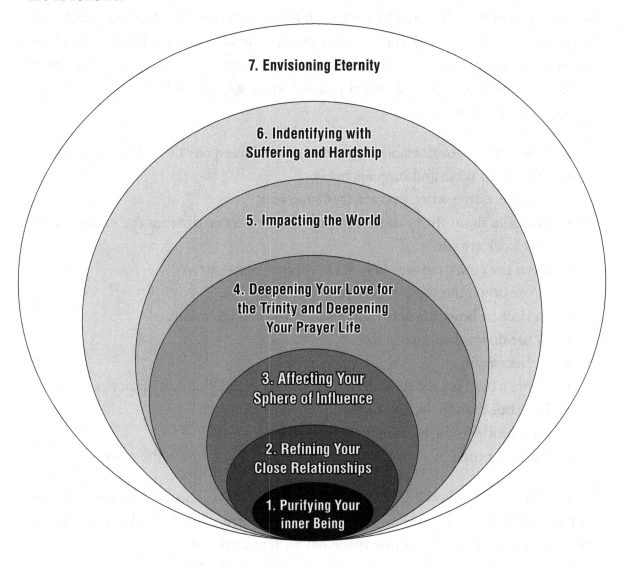

1. Purifying your inner being:_____
2. Refining your close relationships:_____
3. Affecting your sphere of influence:_____
4. Deepening your love for the Trinity and deepening your prayer life:

   _____

5. Impacting the world:_____
6. Identifying with suffering and hardship:_____
7. Envisioning eternity:_____

Rest Stop: Homework Time

It's homework time once again, and this week's homework is my favorite week of all. You will enter into the lives of some of the heroes of the faith of the Old Testament. May you not only be inspired by how each of these heroes relied on the Lord God, but more importantly, may you see your own personal application and step of faith for each day of this study. God has five life-changing messages for you! Let them invigorate your inner self and propel you to further growth in Him.

Again, as a reminder:

- Find a quiet, comfortable place in which to have your Daily Retreat sessions.
- Have your Bible and supplies ready.
- Choose a time when you are fresh and alert.
- Set aside about thirty minutes or maybe a bit more time for the extra reading this week entails.
- Read the entire passage before choosing a verse or two.
- Write down the verse that pops out at you.
- Reflect on how this verse applies to your own life today.
- Write down that application.
- Reflect again.
- Write a brief prayer about how you will personally put into practice what you have been taught by the Lord.
- Give a title to the message you received from God.
- End your time in awe at God's involvement in your own life today.

Do this for five days before proceeding forward—each day's message is truly inspiring. Ideally, you could do this in one week's time, but if it takes a bit longer, that's OK too. Just keep pursuing this habit with enthusiasm.

You've got this. We'll reconvene when you are finished.

CHAPTER 7 HOMEWORK DAY 1: HEROES OF THE FAITH

Date:

Prayer: Lord, let me tune in to the call You have on my life. Amen.
Passage: 1 Samuel 3:1–21
Title: (insert at end of session)

Verse(s):

Personal Application:

Prayer:

Title: (reinsert at top of page)

The Lord Calls You by Name!

"Cindy, Cindy!" There is something exciting about hearing your name called out in a crowd, isn't there? We wonder, "Who knows me?" as we search for a familiar face with whom we might have friendly fellowship amid a sea of strangers.

As you and I commune with Father God, Jesus Christ, and the Holy Spirit, it will become habit to hear our own, meaningful names spoken aloud to us by the Creator of the world Himself, because we are His own beloved souls with whom He desires to relate.

Write your own name in the following two blanks:

"_____, _____"

Being called by name in a loving tone should be music to your ears. Father God longs to develop this one-on-one rapport with you, just as He did with Samuel, Moses, and all of His beloved intimates, teaching you about Him, along with communicating His high aspirations for you.

Jesus Christ, speaking about His remaining few cherished followers of the Church of Sardis, said,

> Yet you have a few people in Sardis who have not soiled their clothes. They will walk with Me, dressed in white, for they are worthy. The one who is victorious will, like them, be dressed in white. I will never blot out the name of that person from the book of life, but will acknowledge that name before My Father and His angels. (Revelation 3:4–5 NIV)

Your name and mine are known for all eternity. Jesus knows us by our names and is proud to speak our names before Father God and His angels. Get used to being on a first-name basis with Jesus, the one whose own name is above all other names ever to have been spoken.

> In your relationships with one another, have the same mindset as Christ Jesus: Who, being in very nature God, did not consider equality with God something to be used to His own advantage; rather, He made himself nothing by taking the very nature of a servant, being made in human likeness. And being found in appearance as a man, He humbled himself by becoming obedient to death—even death on a cross! Therefore God exalted him to the highest place and gave Him

the Name that is above every name, that at the Name of Jesus every knee should bow, in heaven and on earth and under the earth, and every tongue acknowledge that Jesus Christ is Lord, to the glory of God the Father. (Philippians 2:5–8 NIV)

I'm awestruck that our very own names are on the lips of Jesus Christ. Aren't you, too?

CHAPTER 7 HOMEWORK DAY 2: HEROES OF THE FAITH

Date:

Prayer: Lord, what sacrifice of obedience are You asking of me? If I do so, what will be the outcome? Amen.
Passage: Genesis 22:1–19
Title: (insert at end of session)

Verse(s):

Personal Application:

Prayer:

Title: (reinsert at top of page)

MY WILLING OBEDIENCE BRINGS ABOUT GOD'S PROVISION AND BLESSING

God loves to show Himself to you and me through the many mighty acts He does on our behalf. He also loves to challenge us to allow Him to do so by giving us wild assignments that will prove His power and capability in our lives. This is the type of assignment that was given to God's faithful follower Abraham:

> Then God said, "Take your son, your only son, whom you love—Isaac—and go to the region of Moriah. Sacrifice him there as a burnt offering on a mountain I will show you." (Genesis 22:2)

This extreme assignment became a prime foreshadowing (or picture) of what God Himself would do with His own beloved one and only Son, Jesus Christ. Jesus would indeed become our final sacrifice for sin.

> But when this Priest [Jesus] had offered for all time one sacrifice for sins, He sat down at the right hand of God, and since that time He waits for His enemies to be made His footstool. For by one sacrifice He has made perfect forever those who are being made holy. (Hebrews 10:10–12)

How did Abraham respond to this divine assignment? He got up the next morning and went to Mount Moriah with Isaac. Obedience was Abraham's strongest characteristic. Why on earth would he obey that assignment? He knew God would show Himself in a mighty way by providing a lamb, or substitute, for Isaac, or God would raise Isaac from the dead. This is evident in his words to his servant—"We will come back to you" (Genesis 22:5)—and to Isaac, "God Himself will provide the lamb" (Genesis 22:8).

Abraham obediently placed Isaac on the altar atop Mount Moriah—the same location where Jesus Christ would lay down His own life on the cross for you and me, called Golgotha, or Calvary in Jesus's day. Abraham's greatest step of faith ever was all God wanted. The angel of the Lord immediately intervened, providing a ram as the sacrifice instead.

Abraham's willing obedience brought about God's provision and blessing. Will obeying unusual assignments bring about this same provision and blessing in your life as well? I concretely believe it! In fact, I made my own concrete marker, which sits on the porch at the Oury front door, symbolizing God's undeniable provision for us throughout the years, per my husband's employment in the concrete industry. The

Lord has never failed us through all of the ups and downs. He is our great provider and blessing-giver. It truly has been my exciting joy to obey Him in every glorious assignment given to me. Your stories of God's blessings will be numerous too!

Oury Home

Gen. 22:14

The Lord Will
Provide

CHAPTER 7 HOMEWORK DAY 3: HEROES OF THE FAITH

Date:

Prayer: Lord, I want to be committed to You, no matter what happens in my life. I believe You will rescue me when the heat is on. Amen.
Passage: Daniel 3:1–30
Title: (insert at end of session)

Verse(s):

Personal Application:

Prayer:

Title: (reinsert at top of page)

I Won't Bow Down: Staying True to God at All Costs and Jesus: In the Fire with Me

Idol worship of any kind is abhorred by God. During Shadrach, Meshach, and Abednego's time in Babylonian captivity, citizens of Babylon, along with the Jewish prisoners, were forced to worship the golden statue of King Nebuchadnezzar.

Fast-forward to today, when idols of all sorts are worshipped by our generation as well. Any one of us might choose to bow to the idols of our phones, jobs, wealth, entertainers, government, travel, leaders, sports, food, drink, looks, or self-pleasure. When any of these areas of life become more important than our heavenly Father and Savior Jesus, or they dethrone the Holy Spirit's residence in our hearts, "Houston, we've got a problem."

Shadrach, Meshach, and Abednego, commanded to follow the law of bowing down to the golden statue, refused to do so. When threatened with their lives and brought before the king, the three devout Jewish men, who worshipped God alone, said,

> "King Nebuchadnezzar, we do not need to defend ourselves before you in this matter. If we are thrown into the blazing furnace, the God we serve is able to deliver us from it, and He will deliver us from Your Majesty's hand. But even if He does not, we want you to know, Your Majesty, that we will not serve your gods or worship the image of gold you have set up." (Daniel 3:16–18 NIV)

Wow! What a stand of faith. The three friends of God were willing to stay true to Him, the one, true God, regardless of whether it meant their deaths. Believing God to be fully capable of saving them or fully gracious in taking them to heaven, they stepped out in faith, much to their supernatural surprise!

Thrown into the fiery furnace, which immediately crisped to a crackly crunch the guards who threw them in, the faith of these willing worshippers of God Almighty brought this result instead:

> Then King Nebuchadnezzar leaped to his feet in amazement and asked his advisers, "Weren't there three men that we tied up and threw into the fire?" They replied, "Certainly, Your Majesty." He said, "Look! I see four men walking around in the fire, unbound and unharmed, and the fourth looks like a son of the gods." (Daniel 3:24–25 NIV)

Biblical scholars say that Jesus Himself accompanied the trio into the fire, creating a fearsome foursome. I believe it. I also believe Jesus transformed their bodies into their resurrected state for the moments they were in the fire, thus allowing them to come out unscathed and smelling fresh! I believe Jesus gifts supernatural surprises to those who willingly suffer for His name, rather than double-crossing our defender, proving their greatest faith ever in God alone.

CHAPTER 7 HOMEWORK DAY 4: HEROES OF THE FAITH

Date:

Prayer: Lord, You are the slayer of the giants in my life. I list them now and will face them, knowing You are there. Amen.
Passage: 1 Samuel 17:1–58
Title: (insert at end of session)

Verse(s):

Personal Application:

Prayer:

Title: (reinsert at top of page)

DIVIDED HEART SYNDROME VERSUS FULLY DEVOTED AND READY TO WIN

Throughout the history of God's chosen people, Israel, the nation, suffered from divided heart syndrome. The people, depending on the leadership or mood of the day, would either follow God wholeheartedly or, more often than not, succumb to the temptations surrounding them. Such was the case with King Saul's army, a band of namby-pamby lightweights who faced the mighty Philistine warriors—huge in both size and ego.

Enter young David on the scene. A teenaged shepherd, he was sold out fully to God alone. His heart was singly purposed to follow God, wherever and whenever He told David to go. What made David's heart so undivided, fully devoted, and ready to win? David had seen God work in his life many times. God had helped David kill wild animals—lions and bears—which threatened the sheep. David had even written a thank-you poem, Psalm 23, to God for His constant care of him in every dark and scary situation that a teen might experience as a tender of the flocks in the hilly wilds of Israel.

As David obediently brought food to his brothers on the front lines and heard the taunts of Goliath—a nine-foot-tall giant—he was aghast that the divided hearts within the Israelite army would allow this huge Philistine windbag to defy his living God. These wavering warriors were caving to the god of fear, basing their reality on their adverse circumstances instead of on the God of all resources. Singlehandedly, the emboldened teen questioned the cowardice of these hesitant followers of Yahweh.

> "Who is this uncircumcised Philistine that he should defy the armies of the living God?" (1 Samuel 17:26b NIV)

Singlehandedly, this sold-out soul grabbed the chance to live out his faith in God. David's tenacity, paired with his past experience and topped off with God's empowerment, created an unstoppable trifecta. With only a sling and a stone, David and God together felled Goliath and restored to God the honor due His name. The army, revved up by the victory, annihilated the rest of the Philistine troops, regaining their hope in the God of possibilities through the modeling of one fully devoted follower, the young shepherd David.

How about you and me? Where do we fall on the continuum, where *divided heart* is at one end, and *fully devoted* is at the other end?

Divided heart

Fully devoted

May you and I be unafraid to slay the giants that taunt us in our lives, with the help of God, who stands with us. Our own perseverance, plus our past experiences, along with God's empowerment will make victory possible and count us among the fully devoted few!

CHAPTER 7 HOMEWORK DAY 5: HEROES OF THE FAITH

Date:

Prayer: Lord, I put my faith in You. Answer my prayers, and show me Yourself today. Amen.

Passage: 1 Kings 18:1–40

Title: (insert at end of session)

Verse(s):

Personal Application:

Prayer:

Title: (reinsert at top of page)

ANSWERED PRAYER: WHEN MY FAITH IN GOD BENEFITS ANOTHER

The life of faith that you and I live day by day is not only for our own benefit. We are faithful followers of God to show Him to those who do not yet know Him. God has given us faith in Him so that we might give Him to those without faith.

Such was the case with Elijah versus the evil King Ahab and the 450 false prophets of Baal, whom King Ahab held in high regard. Elijah first called out Ahab's neglect of God and then challenged him to a dual, of sorts. They would test who was the true God—the Lord God or Baal. The one who would send fire to consume the sacrifice would most certainly be God. King Ahab agreed.

In the comical scene that followed, the prophets of Baal called on Baal to light the sacrifice with fire. Nothing happened. Elijah offered some possibilities as to why it had not happened. Perhaps he was napping, working elsewhere, or off seeing the sights of the world. Yep, Baal remained silent.

Elijah, trusting in God's power and ability, dug a trench around his altar and drenched his own sacrifice in gallons of water, which filled up the trench. Knowing the gravity of the situation and that he absolutely needed God to show up, Elijah prayed fervently:

> "Lord, the God of Abraham, Isaac and Israel, let it be known today that you are God in Israel and that I am your servant and have done all these things at your command. Answer me, Lord, answer me, so these people will know that you, Lord, are God, and that you are turning their hearts back again." Then the fire of the Lord fell and burned up the sacrifice, the wood, the stones and the soil, and also licked up the water in the trench. When all the people saw this, they fell prostrate and cried, "The Lord—he is God! The Lord—he is God!" (1 Kings 18:36–39 NIV)

God was gracious to answer Elijah's prayer. God was also gracious to the Israelites, who were watching this showdown, wanting them to know that He is the one, true God who outperforms anything and anyone. Elijah's extreme faith in Yahweh's willingness to answer prayer was rewarded, not only for his own benefit but for the benefit of those onlookers who were in the dark about God in the first place because God stops at nothing to draw people to Him.

Let us pray that when people meet us, they will comprehend our faith in God, who answers prayer. May seeing God in our lives give people the interest and excitement to have God in their lives too.

MAY YOU HEAR CLEARLY WHY JESUS HAS CALLED YOU TO RETREAT WITH HIM DAILY

I hope you enjoyed spending time with Jesus and some of the heroes of our faith this week. How inspiring to see God's interest, power, equipping, and blessing in the lives of Samuel, Abraham, Shadrach, Meshach, Abednego, David, and Elijah and then to experience the faith each one had in the Lord God Almighty in the face of extreme adversity.

My prayer for you is that you will continue to spend time with Jesus regularly for the next three chapters and that you will discern His call on your life. You've already heard from Him, inviting you to seek Him out. Now, I pray you are hearing His reasons why He called you to this intimate practice. Perhaps these are some of the reasons:

- He loves you beyond measure.
- He treasures your personality and unique expressions of portraying Christ to others.
- He wants to confide in you regarding your partnership with Him.
- He desires that your faith be increased for difficulties to come.
- He wants to show you His power over your adversity.
- He knows you are good seed and will produce a crop thirty-, sixty-, or one-hundred-fold.
- He has called, chosen, and appointed you for a fruitful life in the kingdom of God, here on earth.
- He has your name written in His book of life and will see that you reach His kingdom via the path of life He has chosen just for you.

Stay the course, and you will soon discern why you are called to be with Jesus, devotedly, forevermore!

DAILY RETREAT EVALUATION

1. **What worked for you?**

2. **What did not work for you? What was difficult? What needs to change?**

3. **Pray over the difficulties together with God.**

4. **What did you learn? How did the Lord speak to you or use you?**

5. **What excites you? What are your hopes?**

TRAIL AT THE NORTH RIM, GRAND CANYON NATIONAL PARK, ARIZONA

8

LIFE IN THE FAST LANE

TRAVELING IN FIFTH GEAR

My prayer is that, by now, you see Daily Retreats as valuable to your life. You contemplate scripture more than ever before and see its pertinent application to your life. Your perspective on the scope, importance, and necessity of your place in the world has been heightened. Thank you for staying the course. "Well done, good and faithful servant!" (Matthew 25:21a NIV).

Now, in chapter 8, we will learn how to stay on top of our journey with Jesus. There are five powerful ways we may always travel smoothly in fifth gear down the road of life, even when the road gets bumpy. When incorporated regularly, these five practices will prevent stall-outs and accidents along the way. The five habits to stay on track are:

1. Accept yourself for who you are.
2. Seek forgiveness.
3. Forgive readily.
4. Obey completely.
5. Let God navigate.

The difficulty with this chapter is that some of these concepts are hard to accept because they bring up pain. If you recall our earlier discussion on unloading refuse from our lives, you will see the need to approach these five important principles with openness and willingness.

Jesus is all about bringing healing to the places where it's needed. He desires for each of us to allow Him to tweak us, imploring that we trust Him as He works His miracle of brand-new hearts and brand-new minds in us.

When incorporated fully into one's life, the transformative result of these five practices is inner health and outer effectiveness. Welcome to life in the fast lane!

HABIT ONE: ACCEPT YOURSELF FOR WHO YOU ARE

In the refining process, it is easy to get discouraged and think we have to work on too much to ever be acceptable to God or anyone else. The truth is that God made you in His image and loves you just the way He made you, even if you never were to change at all.

> For you created my inmost being; you knit me together in my mother's womb. I praise you because I am fearfully and wonderfully made; your works are wonderful, I know that full well. (Psalm 139:13–14 NIV)

He gave you a unique set of gifts and personality traits that only you have. Appreciate these gifts and offer them to God. Your willingness incites a beautiful transformation from a lump of coal to a dazzling diamond.

> My dove, my perfect one, is unique. (Song of Solomon 6:9 NIV)

ON THE WANTED! LIST

There is nothing like reading a lengthy list of names you can't pronounce for a fun time, is there? Here's an example from 1 Chronicles 4:34–36 (NIV):

> Meshobab, Jamlech, Joshah son of Amaziah, Joel, Jehu son of Joshibiah, the son of Seraiah, the son of Asiel, also Elioenai, Jaakobah, Jeshohaiah, Asaiah, Adiel, Jesimiel, Benaiah …

Who really cares, right? Wrong! Although we don't know who any of these individuals were or what they did, God chose each person to be born, live, and have meaning. God needed each and every one of them. He gave each of these people free will and free access to Him. These people were *wanted*!

Have you ever given much thought about your own genealogy? How did you come to be *you*? Who was in your past? Without them, good or bad, you would not be here.

I have my own unique little story in my genealogy. My maternal grandmother was her parents' tenth child. Her mother had five boys followed by five girls. Now, *that* is a crowded covered-wagonload of kids, which is exactly how they came to Colorado. But what if my great-grandmother had stopped having children at number nine? Nine children would be plenty, right?

Wrong! If my grandmother, the treasured tenth child, had not been born, there are now thirty-eight people who would not have been born either—including my mother, my two sisters, my niece in heaven, my niece and her children, my nephew, me, my six sensational children, and my eight precious grandchildren (including twins who died in utero), not to mention my aunt, cousins, and their children and grandchildren. Yes, my grandmother Golda was indeed *wanted* by God—and by me!

You are wanted by all of those who follow after you for decades to come. Without you, there wouldn't be them! Those who are single are also wanted by all of those they touch with their gifts, used to make this world a better place.

Yes, married or single, children or no children, you are definitely wanted, needed, and cherished by God and by those who have been blessed by your presence in their lives. I am one of them. Thank you for partnering with Jesus and me in this quest to learn of your great significance to Him and to this world. Continue in service to our Lord Jesus Christ for His glory and for the blessings of those in your sphere of influence. I'm thanking God, along with you, that we are all wanted and needed by Him.

HABIT TWO: SEEK FORGIVENESS

It pleases God when we are humble and contrite regarding our personal sin. Heartfelt confession to Him and those we have wronged keeps our slates clean. He is faithful to forget the sin and remember it no more, and He desires that we be set free from any guilt that would bog us down. Accept this freeing gift of forgiveness.

Drink in the richness of His merciful grace:

> If we confess our sins, he is faithful and just and will forgive us our sins and purify us from all unrighteousness. (1 John 1:9 NIV)

> "If My people, who are called by My name, will humble themselves and pray and seek My face and turn from their wicked ways, then I will hear from heaven, and I will forgive their sin and will heal their land." (2 Chronicles 7:14 NIV)

STRIPPED AND BARE, WITH NOTHING TO HIDE

Nothing was fun about God's judgment on the evil times and practices during the days of the prophets Micah and Isaiah. The northern kingdom of Israel was exiled to Assyria due to their unspeakable defilement of God's standard for living, which was simply "to act justly, to love mercy, and to walk humbly with God" (Micah 6:8b NIV).

Not only did God judge Israel, but He soon would judge the southern kingdom of Judah for their own abhorrent lifestyle and treatment of others.

During this time the prophet Isaiah was given an interesting assignment:

> At that time the Lord spoke through Isaiah, son of Amoz. He said to him, "Take off the sackcloth from your body and the sandals from your feet." And Isaiah did so, going around stripped and barefoot. (Isaiah 20:2 NIV)

Because I am all about "personal application," I pondered this, remembering the time when I came to the spiritual bottom of myself, stripped of my pride and wallowing in the sadness of my personal sin. It was a horrible experience but one I had to have in order to rise up from the pit to my freedom in Christ, who took my shame away for good.

Coming out of judgment into a transformed life is what the Christian message is all about. There is no shame in realizing our shame and thus rising up as a new creation in Christ.

Let us then be stripped bare in the confession of our sins before the Lord our God so that we may be forgiven, then one day exalted forevermore.

HABIT THREE: FORGIVE READILY

Just as we desire God's forgiveness, so others desire our forgiveness. Saying goodbye to grudges, bitterness, anger, and indifference keeps the heart light so we can soar to greater places.

> Be kind and compassionate to one another, forgiving each other, just as in Christ God forgave you. (Ephesians 4:32 NIV)

> "And when you stand praying, if you hold anything against anyone, forgive them, so that your Father in heaven may forgive you your sins." (Mark 11:25 NIV)

NOT WRONG TO BE WRONGED

The only television I tend to watch is the ten o'clock news, and the commercials at that time of night tend to be lawyers promoting their firms and urging people to call them with their civil cases against others. I could give you a list of these lawyers by name, and I'd bet you could do so too. In fact, these lawyer-hounds even got into my son's head when he was only four years old.

Tom had been watching a local television channel that showed both cartoons and commercials. One day after watching his afternoon cartoon, he came to me and asked if we could go to Six Flags Elitch Gardens (an amusement park in Denver, Colorado). Bending down lovingly to look him in the eye, I told him that going to Elitch's was a special treat, and we did not have the money to do it on a normal basis. Tom looked me right back in the eye and said in all seriousness, "Mommy, call Joe Schmoe. He'll get you the money you deserve!"

Apparently, Joe's ancestors were from Corinth, as civil lawsuits were all too common there as well. The apostle Paul was quite perturbed with the Corinthian believers who felt entitled to have their days in court against their fellow brothers and sisters in Christ. Paul writes,

> The very fact that you have lawsuits among you means you have been completely defeated already. Why not rather be wronged? Why not rather be cheated? Instead, you yourselves cheat and do wrong, and you do this to your brothers and sisters! (1 Corinthians 6:7–8 NIV)

Wait a minute—is getting what I "deserve" a defeatist attitude? Really? And then Paul has the audacity to urge us to accept being wronged or cheated? Hmmm. This mindset does not come easily or naturally to any of us. It comes supernaturally. And the following verse tells us how:

> But you were washed, you were sanctified, you were justified in the name of the Lord Jesus Christ and by the Spirit of our God. (1 Corinthians 6:11 NIV)

With the help of the Holy Spirit, you and I may accept being wronged with grace. The greater temperaments to employ are love, forgiveness, and trust in God.

You and I can now adjust our mindsets to match the Lord's in being willing to be wronged, thus forgiving those who have trespassed against us.

HABIT FOUR: OBEY COMPLETELY

We are in obedience training! As we are trained in this habit, we may get small assignments such as, "Don't go over the speed limit," or "Scrape all the snow off every window before driving." Listen closely as Jesus gives many of these assignments every day. They may seem irritating or even maddening, but He is testing our sensitivity to His direction. Are you willing to be inconvenienced by the assignments He gives? Each assignment, small or great, is always in our best interest to obey—He loves us that much.

Take in these rich nuggets of truth regarding obedience:

> His mother said to the servants, "Whatever Jesus says to you, do it!"
> (John 2:5 NASB)

> Give me understanding, so that I may keep your law and obey it with
> all my heart. (Psalm 119:34 NIV)

OBEYING ASSIGNMENTS: AVOIDING VS. PERSEVERING

We are nearly finished with this huge assignment of learning how to spend quality, life-changing time with Jesus. Congratulations! Have you seen God at work through your efforts?

Please do not get discouraged—the conquest is nearly complete. The Lord Jesus will continue to equip you for any remaining battles ahead, both before you finish this training and afterwards as well. He calls you to victory and helps you to achieve it.

Tough assignments like this are easy to quit. Why should we go on, anyway? What is the point? Yet none of us ever really knows God's entire purpose of an assignment until it is concluded. That is why each of us must keep going and persevering.

Jonah was an Old Testament prophet who did not want to perform his assignment from God because it was too personal. Jonah selfishly wanted to keep God to himself by avoiding a people group who were his polar opposites in their morals and practices. Yet how could the Ninevites (pronounced *Nin*-eh-vites) believe if they were not told about the one, true God in the first place? Thus, God assigned Jonah to be His missionary.

Jonah couldn't stomach the thought. In fact, he ran in the opposite direction from it, boarding a ship setting sail for Tarshish—about as far away from Nineveh as a person could get. Yet God would see Jonah through, rearranging Jonah's circumstances so that Jonah would become trapped in the belly of a whale, where he was forced to reconsider his sour stomach toward God and God's assignment for Jonah.

I hope you and I will be reenergized to complete the assignment of developing the Daily Retreat habit in our lives forevermore. There is great reward for such diligence—unless, of course, we sidestep the finish line, as Jonah tried to do.

Together, let us be obediently determined in our assignments, day by day, minute by minute.

HABIT FIVE: LET GOD NAVIGATE

Often, we have an agenda for where we ought to go or what kind of scenery we prefer. Yet when we trust God, He takes us to places we would never expect and shows us things we have never seen. Be adventurous with God.

"For I know the plans I have for you," declares the Lord, "plans to prosper you and not to harm you, plans to give you hope and a future. Then you will call on Me and come and pray to Me, and I will listen to you. You will seek Me and find Me when you seek Me with all your heart." (Jeremiah 29:11–13 NIV)

THE "YEA, GOD" AND "NAY, GOD" CYCLE

In the book of Judges in the Old Testament, the Israelites followed a very unhealthy pattern that led to directionless living:

1. The people wanted to do their own thing and live their own way.
2. Unrighteous life choices and the resulting trouble caused them to cry out to God.
3. God heard, intervened, and rescued them from harm.
4. Life was good again, and soon, old habits and unrighteous living returned.

(Cycle back to points two through four forever.)

How does this same cycle play out in our lives? When times are good, we live carefree lives, the way we want to do. When times are hard, we turn to God. After receiving His help, we are quickly on our way to piloting our lives into the wide blue yonder. This sort of cycle does not bode well with God, who desires to sit solely on the throne of our hearts forever. If Jesus Christ is our Lord and Savior, then the Holy

Spirit has already moved in and has unpacked His bags to stay. Yet without regular monitoring, we might push Him aside and usurp the throne ourselves.

The apostle Paul saw this "Yea, God" and "Nay, God" cycle in the lives of the people of Corinth and urged them to stop. Here is his plea for them to live only a "Yea, God" life:

> Does Christ go strolling with the Devil? Do trust and mistrust hold hands? Who would think of setting up pagan idols in God's holy Temple? But that is exactly what we are, each of us a temple in whom God lives. God himself put it this way:
>
> "I'll live in them, move into them; I'll be their God and they'll be my people. So leave the corruption and compromise; leave it for good," says God. "Don't link up with those who will pollute you. I want you all for myself ..."
>
> With promises like this to pull us on, dear friends, let's make a clean break with everything that defiles or distracts us, both within and without. Let's make our entire lives fit and holy temples for the worship of God. (2 Corinthians 6:15–17; 7:1 MSG)

This lifestyle is not easy. Jesus called it the *narrow gate*. Yet the rewards of allowing God to sit in the driver's seat are blessing and favor, as well as seeing our lives gain momentum!

REST STOP: HOMEWORK TIME

After learning about the five habits of a person who lives life in the fast lane, let's now move forward into our homework portion of the chapter. For the next five days, the homework passages center on each of the five habits discussed. The reflection scripture has already been chosen for you, but the surrounding verses will enhance your understanding of each of the scriptures to be reflected upon.

Remember, Jesus loves you and has chosen you to be His partner in life. He has called you to be His intimate follower. There is no better way to do that than to have these five principles firmly embedded in your mind. Imagine the possibilities that expand before you. Where will you and Jesus go from here?

You know the drill! Take quality time during this portion of the expedition. Pull off to the scenic overlook; then permit Jesus to show you the view He has for your own particular pilgrimage with Him.

See you again very soon on the other side of the homework.

CHAPTER 8 HOMEWORK DAY 1: WHERE WILL JESUS AND I GO FROM HERE?

Date:

Theme: God loves me and created me.
Prayer: Father God, may I see myself as Your wonderful creation.
Passage: Psalm 139
Title: (insert at end of session)

Verse:

> For You created my inmost being; You knit me together in my mother's womb. I praise You because I am fearfully and wonderfully made; Your works are wonderful; I know that full well. (Psalm 139:13–14)

Personal Application:

Prayer:

Title: (reinsert at top of page)

YOU: ORIGINAL, UNIQUE

Newsflash: There is only one Y-O-U!

While this is not really news, it is a rare occasion when we dwell for more than a moment on this fantastic thought. After reading Psalm 139, the obvious assignment is to spend time with God on the subject of Y-O-U: You—Original—Unique. Here are the truths spoken about Y-O-U in Psalm 139. Reopen your Bible, and see these inspiring truths for yourself.

1. God knows all about Y-O-U (Psalm 139:1–4).
2. God protects Y-O-U (verses 5–6).
3. God is with Y-O-U wherever Y-O-U go (verses 7–12).
4. God created Y-O-U uniquely and purposefully (verses 13–15).
5. God knows how many days Y-O-U will live on earth (verse 16).
6. God never stops thinking about Y-O-U (verses 17–18).
7. God wins in the end and thus, Y-O-U win too (verses 19–22).
8. God perfects Y-O-U and moves Y-O-U forward with Him. (verses 23–24).

Spend time reflecting with God about why Y-O-U are here and where He desires to take Y-O-U today, this week, this year, and for the rest of your life. God has invested everything in Y-O-U. Humbly stand tall and believe it!

CHAPTER 8 HOMEWORK DAY 2: WHERE WILL JESUS AND I GO FROM HERE?

Date:

Theme: God has forgiven me completely.
Prayer: Thank you, Lord, for Your mind-boggling forgiveness of my sins.
Passage: 1 John 1:1–2:2
Title: (insert at end of session)

Verse:

> If we confess our sins, He is faithful and just to forgive us our sins and
> to cleanse us from all unrighteousness. (1 John 1:9)

Personal Application:

Prayer:

Title: (reinsert at top of page)

THE TRUTH ABOUT SIN

The apostle John writes the truth about sin:

> If we claim to be without sin, we deceive ourselves and the truth is not in us. If we confess our sins, he is faithful and just and will forgive us our sins and purify us from all unrighteousness. If we claim we have not sinned, we make him out to be a liar and his word is not in us. My dear children, I write this to you so that you will not sin. But if anybody does sin, we have an advocate with the Father—Jesus Christ, the Righteous One. He is the atoning sacrifice for our sins, and not only for ours but also for the sins of the whole world. (1 John 1:8–2:2 NIV)

1. **Any human has sinned and will sin** (1 John 1:8). To be without sin is to be Jesus Christ. So I must stay truthful and realize I am a sinner.
2. **God's word says I have sinned** (verse 10). All my "righteousness" is as filthy rags (Isaiah 64:6 NIV) on my own. I need forgiveness and empowerment to overcome sin, by way of Jesus Christ.
3. **My repentance and confession are key factors to restoration** (verse 9). Repentance means being sorry that I have offended God by my poor attitude or choice. If I confess my sin, naming and claiming it, God is faithful and just to forgive my sin and to cleanse me from my unrighteousness.
4. **The key to forgiveness is my advocate, Jesus Christ** (verse 2:1b). Jesus Christ, the righteous one, has paid the price for my sin. His once-and-for all sacrifice on the cross deems me "white as snow" (Isaiah 1:18 NIV). This is the amazing grace of God.
5. **Jesus is the good news for you, for me, and for the whole world** (verse 2:2). Jesus is the atoning sacrifice for my sins and also the sins of the whole world.

When you or I sin, it might take only a few seconds to get back on track. "Oh no, I forgot to tell my friend that I will be late to our coffee time. Let me text right now, as You brought it to my mind. Then I will not cause my friend to wonder or worry. I love Your promptings. Amen!"

Perhaps it will take a bit longer to rectify. "Oh no! I forgot to put the trash out again! Help me get a better plan, Lord, because forgetfulness does not please You. Hmmm. Yes, I could write it on my calendar. Yes, I could also put a note on my front door every Wednesday that says, 'Put the trash out Wednesday night!' Thank you, Lord. Yes, I will go right now and do those two assignments."

The fix might even be a larger investment of time. "I continue to struggle with this personal issue. I don't like the effects it has on my family, Lord. Help me to be brave and confess this to them. Perhaps I need professional counsel or some other action You tell me to take. Let me no longer sweep this under the rug. I realize that things can only get better once I take action on my sin. Father God, You are oh-so-good to me. I have new hope for getting back on track with You and my family, with Your help, even if it takes several months of concentrated effort. Amen."

Prompt action to sweeping sin out from our souls is pleasing to God and promises quick restoration to life in the fast lane.

REMEMBER TO EMPLOY THE REPENTANCE AND RESTORATION CYCLE

Once again, any time you or I sin, falling short of God's best for us, we may take the steps in the repentance/restoration cycle (see the diagram on the next page) to quickly reestablish our connection to Father God.

1. Recognize my sin.
2. Repent of my sin.
3. Confess my sin to God in prayer.
4. Comprehend that Jesus Christ atoned for my sin through His death and Resurrection, doing for me that which I cannot do for myself.
5. Receive God's forgiveness.
6. Receive God's white-as-snow cleansing.
7. Comprehend the unmerited favor that has been given to me freely, move forward in faith, and seek the restoration necessary to rectify the situation for a complete repair.

May repentance and restoration be a regular part of your life and mine. Let us live forgiven, cleansed, and empowered through our advocate, Jesus. Amen!

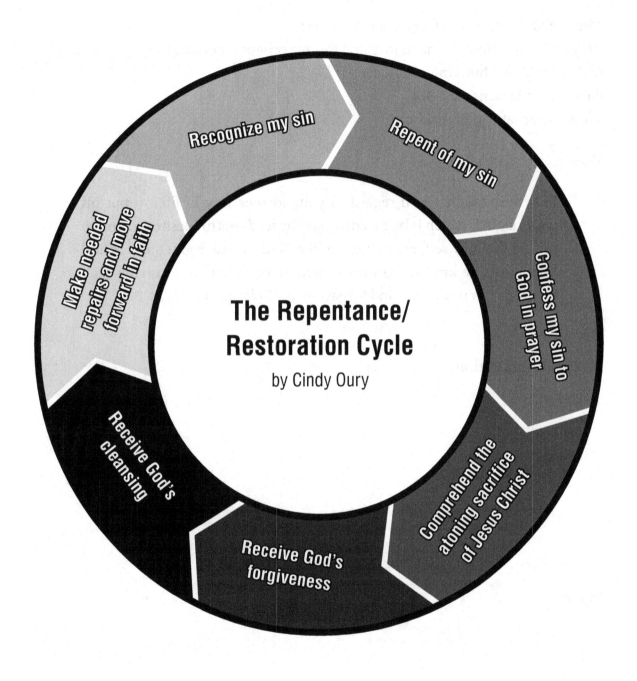

Recognize my sin

Repent of my sin

Confess my sin to God in prayer

Make needed repairs and move forward in faith

The Repentance/ Restoration Cycle

by Cindy Oury

Comprehend the atoning sacrifice of Jesus Christ

Receive God's cleansing

Receive God's forgiveness

CHAPTER 8 HOMEWORK DAY 3: WHERE WILL JESUS AND I GO FROM HERE?

Date:

Theme: Give the gift of forgiveness to others.
Prayer: Jesus, empower me to love and forgive others supernaturally, as it is difficult to do in my own humanity. Amen.
Passage: Ephesians 4:20–32
Title: (insert at end of session)

Verse:

> You were taught, with regard to your former way of life, to put off your old self, which is being corrupted by its deceitful desires … and to put on the new self, created to be like God in true righteousness and holiness … Be kind and compassionate to one another, forgiving each other, just as in Christ, God forgave you. (Ephesians 4:22–24, 32)

Personal Application:

Prayer:

Title: (reinsert at top of page)

EMPOWERED TO BESTOW SUPERNATURAL FORGIVENESS

When hearts and minds have been damaged by the hurtful ways of another, it is natural to hold onto bitterness or resentment toward the guilty party. When left unchecked, such feelings impair the health of our own bodies, minds, and spirits. These negative emotions arise from an "old self" response. Paul, in writing to the Ephesians, said,

> You were taught, with regard to your former way of life, to put off your old self, which is being corrupted by its deceitful desires ... and to put on the new self, created to be like God in true righteousness and holiness ... Be kind and compassionate to one another, forgiving each other, just as in Christ God forgave you. (Ephesians 4:22–24, 32 NIV)

You and I may miraculously let go of hostility when the Holy Spirit takes over, and our new, spiritually transformed self releases the negative emotions we thought we wanted to keep, incorporating instead the godly qualities of kindness, compassion, and supernatural forgiveness.

Because we have been forgiven immeasurably, we too forgive others just as remarkably. This is how people around us recognize Christ in you and me—since such a response to mistreatment is extraordinary. Giving up the prison sentence of vindictiveness affords us a further benefit—inner freedom regained. Soar to new heights on the wings of eagles by employing supernatural forgiveness. You will never be held back from all God desires for you again. Amen!

> Those who hope in the Lord will renew their strength. They will soar on wings like eagles; they will run and not grow weary, they will walk and not be faint. (Isaiah 40:31 NIV)

CHAPTER 8 HOMEWORK DAY 4: WHERE WILL JESUS AND I GO FROM HERE?

Date:

Theme: His wish is my command—quick obedience!
Prayer: Jesus, may I be quick to obey what You tell me to do.
Passage: John 2:1–11
Title: (insert at end of session)

Verse:

> Jesus's mother said to the servants, "Whatever He says to you, do it!"
> (John 2:5)

Personal Application:

Prayer:

Title: (reinsert at top of page)

"WHATEVER HE SAYS TO YOU, DO IT" OBEDIENCE

We all know the famous shoe slogan that propels us to get off the couch, put on a pair of great-performing sneakers, and run to the gym, so as to be rewarded with a healthy body. Yet that phrase was originally spoken by Mary, mother of Jesus, who knew the miraculous impact an attitude of quick obedience would have when it came to her Son.

At the wedding feast in Cana, the bride, groom, and family were put in an awkward social situation when the wine ran out. After appealing to Jesus, Mary ordered the servants to just go for it, in response to Jesus's instructions.

> His mother said to the servants, "Whatever He says to you, do it." (John 2:5 NASB)

They did just go for it. Through agreeing to Jesus's oddly preposterous assignment of dipping out freshly poured water from a jug into a carafe and walking it to the headwaiter, their act of obedience allowed the family and guests to experience the best wine anyone on earth has ever tasted, aged for zero minutes by Jesus. The grand miracle occurred as a result of the servants believing and acting on the instructions of the Savior of situations, and somewhere in the midst of obedience, the water changed to wine.

Are you and I up for adopting the phrase, "Whatever He says to you, do it," in our own lives? What might happen if we lived faithfully by these words? First, we'd be asked to do some wacky assignments, given to us at inconvenient times in unexpected places. Second, we would see the fruit of our willingness and obedience as we witnessed firsthand, everyday miracles happening in our spheres of influence. Let's get off the couch, follow the Holy Spirit's leading, and just do whatever He says!

Here's to our adopting "Whatever He says to you, do it" obedience and experiencing more miracles.

CHAPTER 8 HOMEWORK DAY 5: WHERE WILL JESUS AND I GO FROM HERE?

Date:

Theme: Your Adventure with Jesus Awaits!
Prayer: Jesus, You know our future together. May I be changed, shown, used, and sent by You!
Passage: Jeremiah 29:1–14
Title: (insert at end of session)

Verse:

> "For I know the plans I have for you," declares the Lord, "plans to prosper you and not to harm you, plans to give you hope and a future. Then you will call on me and come and pray to me, and I will listen to you. You will seek me and find me when you seek me with all your heart." (Jeremiah 29:11–13)

Personal Application:

Prayer:

Title: (reinsert at top of page)

CONSECRATE YOURSELF—A NEW ERA HAS BEGUN!

After forty years of wandering in the desert, God's chosen people were about to embark on a new era in their history. The Israelites were on the verge of crossing the Jordan River on dry land. God wanted them pure, undefiled, and clean of mind and body to witness the next day's miracle, which He would perform in their midst. He was leading this group, who formerly were a fickle brood of nay-sayers, into a new future, where they would be mighty, faithful followers. The wanderings were over, and entrance into the promised land was about to take place. Joshua's words rang out:

> "Consecrate yourselves, for tomorrow the Lord will do amazing things among you!" (Joshua 3:5 NIV)

Here is the definition of the word *consecration* from *Easton's Bible Dictionary*.[6]

> consecration: the devoting or setting apart of anything to the worship or service of God.

The Lord, our God, asks that we clean ourselves from sin and worldliness. We are to make ourselves ready to see Him work in our midst because He is about to do something incredible! This week's homework has, in essence, prepared you and me to consecrate our lives for the spectacular new adventures God has prepared for us, beginning right now.

> Yet as soon as the priests who carried the ark reached the Jordan and their feet touched the water's edge, the water from upstream stopped flowing … The priests who carried the ark of the covenant of the Lord stopped in the middle of the Jordan and stood on dry ground, while all Israel passed by until the whole nation had completed the crossing on dry ground. (Joshua 3:15–17 NIV)

What awaits us in the promised land of a life dedicated to God's service? Let us walk across the Jordan River on dry ground to boldly find out.

---

[6] *Easton's Bible Dictionary*, "Consecration," accessed December 17, 2023, https://www.biblestudytools.com/dictionaries/eastons-bible-dictionary/consecration.html.

MY PAST PREPARES ME FOR MY FUTURE

What have you or I experienced in life thus far? While sitting with Jesus, I realized that the responsibilities and adventures I had in the past have prepared me for the new assignments He has given me. I created a worksheet to help you see how Jesus Christ might desire to use you in the near future for His purposes.

Fill in the "Past" categories with one- or two-word descriptions. Fill in the "Future" category in the same way. For example, in the past-jobs category, I would fill in "food server, activities director, mom, grandmother, acting teacher, hospice worker." In the "Future" Category I could put "grandmother, hospice worker, author, published playwright."

I carry the roles of grandmother and hospice worker with me into the future from the past. I'm working on *author* right now. *Published playwright* could possibly happen—or not. "What do You think about that, Jesus?"

You, too, sit with Jesus and ask Him to give you a vision for your future in these categories. Add your words in the outer free spaces. Have fun with this. Nothing is set in stone except our Lord and Savior, the Rock!

> Since you are my Rock and my Fortress, for the sake of your name lead and guide me. (Psalm 31:3 NIV)

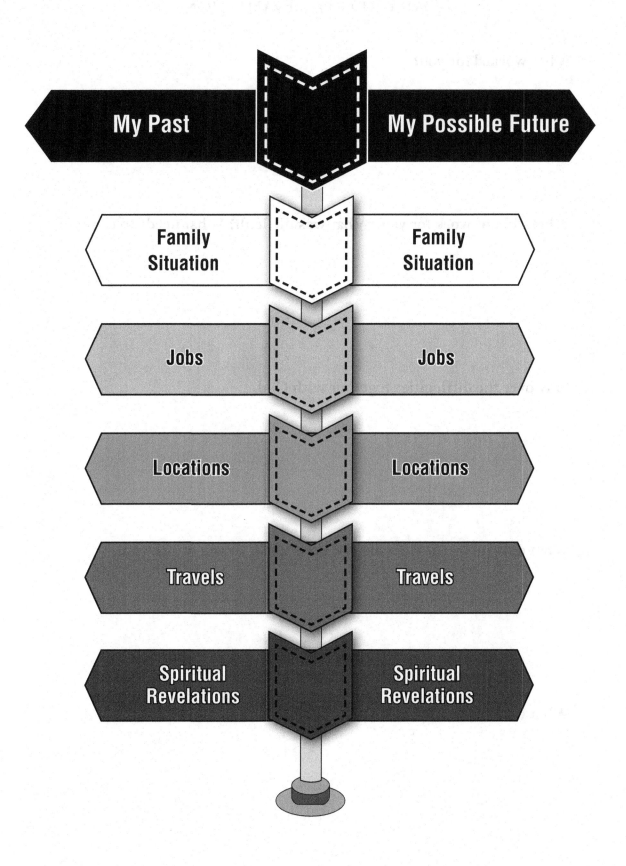

Daily Retreat Evaluation

1. **What worked for you?**

2. **What did not work for you? What was difficult? What needs to change?**

3. **Pray over the difficulties together with God.**

4. **What did you learn? How did the Lord speak to you or use you?**

5. **What excites you? What are your hopes?**

CINDY, STEPPING CAREFULLY ALONG STANLEY CANYON TRAIL, US
AIR FORCE ACADEMY, COLORADO SPRINGS, COLORADO

9

EASY MAINTENANCE

ENDING ONE EXCURSION, PUSHING ON TO THE NEXT

Congratulations! You have accomplished much thus far. Let's reflect for a moment on where we started and how we will finish well these last two chapters of *Your Jesus Journey.*

By far, the most important message of this book is to understand for yourself who Jesus is and that He hopes, more than anything, to have an intimate relationship with you. You saw that Jesus deems you as "flawless," not by your own behavior but because of His perfect life, lived purposely in exchange for your numerous imperfections. In adoration to Him, you offer back the gift of yourself, which begins the greatest power duo to ever hit the planet, Jesus + you.

The expression of your dynamic-duo combo comes through the process of Daily Retreat—quiet contemplation of Jesus's will for you, paired with your obedience to see His will through. Taking time with Him through scripture reflection teaches you much about yourself; you acknowledge that certain inward improvements will always be necessary throughout your life. So, too, you identify various beliefs, behaviors, and practices which usually will prevent your time with the Lord from happening.

It is necessary to adopt a mindset change, comprehending instead the various reasons for incorporating the important practice of Daily Retreat into our routines. Further, we recognize that our partnership with Christ impacts not only ourselves and our families but also our churches, communities, workplaces, and beyond with the love and joy of His presence in us.

Jesus is excited when we develop a healthy outlook about ourselves, accepting the persons He created and maintaining our right relationships with God and our fellow citizens of earth.

The practice of Daily Retreat has truly proven to bring clear mental, emotional, and spiritual health to me throughout the years. By consulting regularly with Jesus, a peaceful, healthy outlook on life, even in the most turbulent of circumstances, may be yours as well.

EASY MAINTENANCE

Taking all of the concepts throughout *Your Jesus Journey* into account, I have found in my forty-plus years of practicing Daily Retreat that the two quickest, easiest actions I should take to maintain forward progress with the Lord are keeping an attitude of reverent humility in approaching our Creator, paired with a swift obedience to do what Jesus says to do at any given moment. I've discussed these two concepts previously, but now, envision them as the bread and wine of your daily existence. Reverent humility plus swift obedience will be your sustenance, resulting in abundant life.

> Then Jesus declared, "I am the bread of life. Whoever comes to me will never go hungry, and whoever believes in me will never be thirsty." (John 6:35 NIV)

> In the same way, after supper he took the cup, saying, "This cup is the new covenant in my blood; do this, whenever you drink it, in remembrance of me." (1 Corinthians 11:25 NIV)

ACTION ONE: REVERENT HUMILITY

Remaining humble before the Lord is the greatest gift you can give to God. It is also your greatest asset because you will reap His rewards. God is drawn to those who put Him first but is very much opposed to those who show no regard for His majesty.

Absorb, through the scriptures, the meaning and result of reverent humility:

> It is the Lord your God you must follow, and him you must revere. Keep his commands and obey him; serve him and hold fast to him. (Deuteronomy 13:4 NIV)

"These are the ones I look on with favor: those who are humble and contrite in spirit, and who tremble at My word." (Isaiah 66:2 NIV)

HYPOCRISY OR HUMILITY?

Jesus was not one to mince words or beat around the bush when it came to issues that offended His Father in heaven. One such matter of contention was the hypocrisy of the elite Pharisees. He blatantly warned the Pharisees of the consequences of their double standards. Woe!

> "Woe to you, teachers of the law and Pharisees, you hypocrites! You are like whitewashed tombs, which look beautiful on the outside but on the inside are full of the bones of the dead and everything unclean. In the same way, on the outside you appear to people as righteous but on the inside, you are full of hypocrisy and wickedness." (Matthew 23:27–28 NIV)

Contrary to displays of hypocrisy, Jesus, just moments before His scathing statements to the pompous Pharisees, urged His own disciples to take on humility instead.

> The greatest among you will be your servant. For those who exalt themselves will be humbled, and those who humble themselves will be exalted. (Matthew 23:11–12 NIV)

Easton's 1897 Bible Dictionary gives this definition of humility:

> A prominent Christian grace *(Rom. 12:3; 15:17, 18; 1 Cor. 3:5-7; 2 Cor. 3:5; Phil. 4:11-13)*. It is a state of mind well-pleasing to God *(1 Pet. 3:4)*; it preserves the soul in tranquility *(Ps. 69:32, 33)*, and makes us patient under trials *(Job 1:22)*. Christ has set us an example of humility *(Phil. 2:6-8)*. We should be led thereto by a remembrance of our sins *(Lam. 3:39)*, and by the thought that it is the way to honor *(Prov. 16:18)*, and that the greatest promises are made to the humble *(Ps. 147:6; Isa. 57:15; 66:2; 1 Pet. 5:5)*. It is a "great paradox in Christianity that it makes humility the avenue to glory.[7]

---

[7] *Easton's Bible Dictionary*, "Humility," accessed December 17, 2023. https://www.biblestudytools.com/dictionaries/eastons-bible-dictionary/humility.

His hatred for hypocrisy and His love for humility were displayed by His own actions, as Jesus put His money where His mouth was:

> After that, he poured water into a basin and began to wash his disciples' feet, drying them with the towel that was wrapped around him … "Now that I, your Lord and Teacher, have washed your feet, you also should wash one another's feet. I have set you an example that you should do as I have done for you." (John 13:5, 14–15 NIV)

Let us allow hardened hypocrisy to hit the road and instead seek reverent humility, our offering to our omnipotent God and in service one to another.

ACTION TWO: SWIFT OBEDIENCE

Reiterated again, obedience to Jesus Christ is your lifeblood—His spirit surging within you—to spill out upon those whom He puts in your path. Growth in all areas of your life will only magnify with each step of faith you take with Him. Jesus is delighted when His close friends trust Him enough to quickly complete the assignments He gives. The rewards reaped from doing so are out of this world!

> If you are willing and obedient, you will eat the good things of the land. (Isaiah 1:19 NIV)

> "Very truly I tell you, whoever obeys my word will never see death." (John 8:51 NIV)

FROM RELUCTANCE TO REVELATION

In 1972–73, during my seventh-grade year, my life science teacher, Mr. Rodney, made a grand impression on all of his students. In white, suburban Arvada, Colorado, he was perhaps the only larger-than-life person of color in town. His formidable presence at the head of the class had us all shaking silently in our seats as he bellowed, in his Southern preacher's voice, the lessons of life science and life in general, as taught to him by his grandpappy, who had worked on the cotton plantations of the South.

In spring, the culmination of the class was the disgusting practice of frog dissection. Using the democratic process of "rock, paper, scissors," the lot and scalpel fell to me. After pinning down the frog's four appendages, I was left to split the abdominal area down the middle with the scalpel. Like Jonah before me, I wanted in the worst way to get on a ship bound for Tarshish. My hesitation, however, lasted a moment too long. From across the room came the roar of Mr. Rodney:

"Adams! I said, Cindy Adams! My grandpappy used to say to me, 'You can lead a horse to water, *but you cannot make him drink*'!"

Snapping out of my fileting phobia, I took the plunge and sliced the belly of the frog. As my lab partners pulled back the flaps, we beheld a most astonishing, intricate, and exquisite world of tiny tubes and geometric shapes, which were stomach, heart, and lungs. My reluctance had turned to wondrous revelation with one obedient swipe of the scalpel.

To what act of obedience is the Lord calling you today? How is reluctance hampering the journey ahead? Spend time with Jesus, listening to, agreeing with, and obeying His every call, as greater revelations than frog innards are yours for the believing. Let's drink the horse's water, quickly and together, shall we?

REST STOP: HOMEWORK TIME

This week's homework is as unique as you are. You will choose your own passages to read and reflect upon. What might you choose to read? Here are some suggestions:

- Pick up where we left off in Matthew. Read chapters 8, 9, 10, 11, and 12, one chapter for each of the five days, choosing a verse to reflect upon each day.
- Or you may start in Matthew 8 and just read a few verses until one verse or story hits you; then reflect on that one. Pick up where you left off for day two.
- Perhaps some of the Bible verses throughout this book have meant something to you. You could find a verse for each day and write about its importance to your life. Find the verse in your own Bible, and underline it.
- The New Testament book of 1 Thessalonians has five chapters. Read it this week, a chapter a day, and find relevant scripture in each chapter on which to reflect.
- Read the book of Ruth in the Old Testament. It has four chapters. Find four purposeful passages, and apply them to your life.
- Read the Gospel of Mark. Start in and stop at the section where you found a significant verse. Continue on that way, just a small portion at a time.
- Do the same as above for the books of Galatians, Ephesians, Philippians, or Colossians in the New Testament.
- Read various Psalms or Proverbs.
- If you are in another Bible study, try dwelling on the verses, Daily Retreat–style.

No need to be fearful; just enjoy exploring the Bible. Choose a Bible verse to reflect on each day, and let Jesus work His miracles in you.

May you be blessed as you strike out on your own this week. Enjoy!

Note: I have chosen to include some observations about the fruits of the Spirit (Galatians 5:22–23) after each of the homework pages. Plus, at the end of this chapter, there are considerations for choosing your own study after you have finished *Your Jesus Journey*.

CHAPTER 9 HOMEWORK DAY 1: MY CHOICE! HERE WE GO, JESUS!

Date:

Prayer:

Passage:

Title: (insert at end of session)

Verse:

Personal Application:

Prayer:

Title: (reinsert at top of page)

Sign Me Up for Sanctification, or the Reward of the Fruit of the Spirit

One of the greatest miracles of the Christian life is true inner change—not just saying, "I'm going to have a good attitude today," but experiencing a transformation of attitude, once and for all, that comes only from God.

What would it be like to replace resentment and bitterness toward another with love? To replace complaining with joy? Anxiety with peace? Crossness with patience? Arrogance with kindness? Malice with goodness? Doubt with faithfulness? Severity with gentleness? Impulsiveness with self-control?

Each positive fruit of the Holy Spirit is the reward of a heart bent on change. The apostle Paul wrote the following words to a group of new Christ-followers in Galatia; these have meant the world to me throughout my walk with Jesus.

> But the fruit of the Spirit is love, joy, peace, patience, kindness, goodness, faithfulness, gentleness and self-control. Against such things there is no law. Those who belong to Christ Jesus have crucified the flesh with its passions and desires. Since we live by the Spirit, let us keep in step with the Spirit. (Galatians 5:22–25 NIV)

This process of sanctification—becoming more and more like Jesus—takes place one day at a time. It begins when I humbly ask God to make me more like Christ through my Daily Retreat time and then purpose to obey His advice throughout the day ahead, as the Holy Spirit assists me to become stronger in my areas of weakness. Jesus's power, through the Holy Spirit, my helper, revolutionizes my soul.

God has extraordinary changes He wants to make and gifts He wants to give when you sign up for sanctification.

CHAPTER 9 HOMEWORK DAY 2: MY CHOICE! HERE WE GO, JESUS!

Date:

Prayer:

Passage:

Title: (insert at end of session)

Verse:

Personal Application:

Prayer:

Title: (reinsert at top of page)

FULL JOY: ABIDING IN CHRIST, THE SOURCE OF JOY

I chuckled at this good news/bad news joke:

> Doctor: I have some good news, and I have some bad news.
> Patient: What's the good news?
> Doctor: The good news is that you have twenty-four hours to live.
> Patient: That's the good news? What's the bad news?
> Doctor: The bad news is that I forgot to call you yesterday.

Not long ago, I experienced my own real-life version of this good news/bad news drama, but I did not find it humorous in the least. In fact, it sent me into a downward spin. How interesting that it happened at the very time I wanted to write about joy.

How do you and I maintain joy, even when circumstances look grim? With firsthand practice, practice, and practice, I can say that focusing on Jesus Christ is the key to living with a light heart in a heavy-hearted situation. In John 15, Jesus says that if we abide in Him, we will be full of the fruit of His joy, which will effervesce from us.

> "I am the vine; you are the branches. If you remain [or abide] in me and
> I in you, you will bear much fruit; apart from me you can do nothing …
> I have told you this so that my joy may be in you and that your joy may
> be complete." (John 15:5, 11 NIV)

Frankly, it takes some concentrated effort to see the good news of Jesus Christ in the bad news of the day. How are you doing with that assignment? Are you able to make sweet lemonade from the sour lemons that roll your way? Do you have that deep, unexplainable joy, joy, joy, joy down in your heart to stay?

Together, let us practice finding His good news in all situations and thus tap into a refreshing drink of the full joy He has already given us.

CHAPTER 9 HOMEWORK DAY 3: MY CHOICE! HERE WE GO, JESUS!

Date:

Prayer:

Passage:

Title: (insert at end of session):

Verse:

Personal Application:

Prayer:

Title: (reinsert at top of page)

REST IN PEACE OR RESIST HIS PEACE?

One commodity that is a shortfall for most of us is rest. Rest comes in many forms, yet there isn't enough to go around.

On the positive side, we may rest for a moment or two during the day, sleep well at night, relax in knowing God is in control, be at peace in our difficult circumstances, and trust that our future is secure.

Of course, we are also free to resist the peaceful rest. We might instead choose to stress out all day long, toss and turn at night, worry and fret over every uncertainty, grumble and complain about our difficult circumstances, and wonder forever if we have done everything correctly for our unknown future.

The Bible says this about God's rest:

> There remains, then, a Sabbath-rest for the people of God; for anyone who enters God's rest also rests from their works, just as God did from his. Let us, therefore, make every effort to enter that rest. (Hebrews 4:9–11 NIV)

The place of ultimate rest and peace still awaits us in heaven. But today we may peacefully encircle ourselves inside the hedge of protection and haven of repose that comes from fully trusting in God. He has gathered us as a hen gathers her chicks and will always be with us. On this fact, let us rest, not resist.

> "Jerusalem, Jerusalem, you who kill the prophets and stone those sent to you, how often I have longed to gather your children together, as a hen gathers her chicks under her wings, and you were not willing." (Matthew 23:37 NIV)

> Finally, brothers and sisters, rejoice! Strive for full restoration, encourage one another, be of one mind, live in peace. And the God of love and peace will be with you. (2 Corinthians 13:11 NIV)

CHAPTER 9 HOMEWORK DAY 4: MY CHOICE! HERE WE GO, JESUS!

Date:

Prayer:

Passage:

Title: (insert at end of session)

Verse:

Personal Application:

Prayer:

Title: (reinsert at top of page)

THE GIFT OF HIS GENTLENESS TOWARD ME

It's nearly the end of the book. Kudos on persevering throughout this study. Congratulations on paving the way to navigating through life triumphantly. Whew— the end of this particular road is in sight. If you feel exhausted or in need of a break at this point or any time the going gets rough, remember you have a gentle giant on your side.

It is interesting that when we are limp from the long haul, Jesus beckons us to come to Him. He says,

> "Come to Me, all who are weary and heavy-laden, and I will give you rest. Take My yoke upon you and learn from Me, for I am gentle and humble in heart, and you will find rest for your souls. For My yoke is easy and My burden is light." (Matthew 11:28–30 NASB)

Jesus makes it clear that He is to bear the brunt of our burdens when we are bankrupt, beaten, breathless, or broken. The help He offers us is to relinquish our loads so that He may carry it Himself. The way we learn this life-changing lesson is to simply to come to Him. We will encounter neither harshness nor condemnation. Instead, we will experience His gentle humility as He relieves us of our cares, resulting in rest from our weariness. This simple practice of coming to Jesus brings solace to our souls.

Will you amass a soul full of serenity by going to the humble, gentle source of refreshment, Jesus?

I'm headed to lay my burdens down right now. Won't you join me?

Chapter 9 Homework Day 5: My Choice! Here We Go, Jesus!

Date:

Prayer:
Passage:
Title (insert at end of session)

Verse:

Personal Application:

Prayer:

Title: (reinsert at top of page)

DRESS FOR SUCCESS: PUT ON LOVE

Like a little black dress, casual khakis, or a soft pair of comfy blue jeans, there are a few traits that we can't be without in our lives as we wear the Lord Jesus on our sleeves. Expounding on the fruit of the spirit of love, Paul urges us to dress for success.

> So, chosen by God for this new life of love, dress in the wardrobe God picked out for you: compassion, kindness, humility, quiet strength, discipline. Be even-tempered, content with second place, quick to forgive an offense. Forgive as quickly and completely as the Master forgave you. And regardless of what else you put on, wear love. It's your basic, all-purpose garment. Never be without it. (Colossians 3:12–14 MSG)

Such rave responses are sure to capture hearts when you step onto the scene! Here are these valuable virtues once again:

- Compassion
- Kindness
- Humility
- Quiet strength
- Discipline
- Even temperament
- Contentment
- Quick to forgive
- Love

These nine adornments to our personalities will keep us in special standing with all those around us and will show the world the charismatic characteristics of Jesus Himself.

Here's to wearing love on the runway and roadway of life!

DAILY RETREAT EVALUATION

1. **What worked for you?**

2. **What did not work for you? What was difficult? What needs to change?**

3. **Pray over the difficulties together with God.**

4. **What did you learn? How did the Lord speak to you or use you?**

5. **What excites you? What are your hopes?**

MAPPING OUT YOUR PERSONAL PLAN OF ACTION

Congratulations on completing the last week of five-day homework for this book. How did it go as you ventured out on your own with Jesus by your side? I hope you felt His encouraging cheer to keep traveling with Him. My prayer is that this beautiful relationship that you two have developed together over these last weeks will continue on forever and beyond. But how will that happen?

For most of us, when we embark on a journey to a distant destination, we plan in advance how we will get there, where we will stay, and what we will do to make the excursion memorable. So it is with Daily Retreat. A plan of action is a necessary component to a successful endeavor.

TRAVEL JOURNAL TIP ONE: CHOOSE YOUR STUDY

What interests you as you think of the Bible as a tool for your life? Choose a self-study with your own interests in mind.

Perhaps you'd like to find out how it all began and dig into the first book of the Bible, Genesis. There are many wonderful and way-out accounts throughout Genesis. You would find out about creation, Adam and Eve, Noah, Abraham, Isaac, Jacob, Jacob's twelve sons, and finally you'd be immersed in the life of Jacob's eleventh son, Joseph, a truly reputable hero of the faith. You would laugh, cry, and be aghast at the behavior of the people God loved, who were called His own, and you'd discover there is much to learn from these real-life humans and even more to absorb about God Himself.

This type of study could take as few as two months or up to six months, if you took it chapter by chapter or passage by passage. The great thing is that you get to decide how slow or fast you go.

Maybe you are more interested in the life of Jesus—what He had to say and what His mission on earth was all about. Then, by all means, choose a Gospel account to study—Matthew, Mark, Luke, or John—all similarly proving Jesus as the awaited Messiah, suffering servant, Savior of the world, and divine Son of God. If you have never read about Jesus, you might begin with Mark. If you want a challenge, read John. You will experience Jesus Himself by reading any or all of them.

The letters, found in the New Testament, give instructions for living. Some of these are Galatians, Ephesians, Philippians, Colossians, and 1 and 2 Peter. You could study one of these books for many applications on how to live a life pleasing to God.

If you currently attend a Bible study, you may adopt the Daily Retreat process as you study your lesson. Break the weekly lesson into three, four, or five days of study. After you look up your verses and answer the questions, take one verse that has popped out at you, and use that verse for your journal time. Or just use this same Bible study book as your journal by writing in the margins. You will have already seen its application for your life and will be able to quickly write down this thought, along with any further insights for your life.

I learned this five-day process by attending Bible Study Fellowship, another great option, for many years in my early walk with Christ. Then I transformed *The Navigators* Lifechange Series Bible study books into journals and divided each weekly lesson into the five-day process I had learned in Bible Study Fellowship.

While I heartily recommend reading the Bible itself for your Daily Retreat time, there have been a handful of times when I have incorporated the Daily Retreat process when reading another author's book. It's necessary, though, that a Christian book of this sort have Bible verse references for the points made.

I would choose one of these verses for reflection and write my personal application in the margins. *The Purpose Driven Life* by Rick Warren (read in forty days, as recommended by the author) and *The Power of a Praying Woman* by Stormie Omartian are two such books I've used in this way.

Whatever you choose, remember that the Holy Spirit's power for your inner transformation comes when you personally apply scripture to your own life. This is the key to sanctifying growth, day by day, one Bible verse at a time.

> The word is very near you; it is in your mouth and in your heart so you may obey it. (Deuteronomy 30:14 NIV)

My study will be:

Travel Journal Tip Two: Set a Goal

Set a realistic goal for yourself, such as, "With God's help, I will have a Daily Retreat three times a week for twenty to thirty minutes a day." This is very doable because if you get sidetracked or something comes up one day, you can find twenty minutes later that day or the next. Even if you cannot keep the same time and place, just find a new time and place for that day. The important focus is a whatever-He-says-to-you-do-it mentality. With God's help, as far as we are able, we will meet the goals we set for ourselves.

"Set up road signs, put up guideposts. Take note of the highway, the road that you take." (Jeremiah 31:21 NASB)

Brothers and sisters, I do not consider myself yet to have taken hold of it. But one thing I do: Forgetting what is behind and straining toward what is ahead, I press on toward the goal to win the prize for which God has called me heavenward in Christ Jesus. (Philippians 3:13–14 NIV)

My goal will be:

TRAVEL JOURNAL TIP THREE: BE ACCOUNTABLE

If your self-discipline has not yet kicked in for this adventure, then get someone to help keep you on track. If you invite the Holy Spirit to take this job, He will! Also, you may want to choose your spouse, friend, prayer partner, Bible study buddy, or a mentor to hold you accountable.

Be creative! Form a support group and meet weekly for encouragement:

In our early twenties BC (before children), my husband, Leo, and I met in a wonderful, young twentysomethings' group with an inspiring mentor couple who had two preschool boys. They lived their faith and displayed to us all what a godly family life looked like. We shared, laughed, and learned the lessons of Jesus Christ together. A lifelong mentorship and enduring friendships were the result.

When I was in my thirties, I met with three other young moms for Bible study from 5:30 a.m. to 6:45 a.m. at each other's homes once a week, leaving our husbands to supervise our young children, toddlers, and babies. My lifelong friendships with them continue, and I still meet regularly with one of them, twenty-seven years later!

During our thirties and forties, Leo and I led a small group for growing families twice a month. We had a blast with five to eight families, all spending the evening together in fellowship, along with a special time of gleaning from the Word of God for both the adults and children. We held each other up in prayer and helped each other through the ups and downs of life.

From 2009 to 2014, I taught my Daily Retreat class for women on Sunday mornings. This support group bloomed, and many women benefited from this close-knit fellowship. Lifelong friendships emerge when life's crucial moments are shared together.

In 2015, Jesus had me begin a deeper Bible study for any who were willing. Many empty-nesters attended. We have had a wonderful support group in this Sunday morning class for nearly a decade and have made it our individual goals to grow in the knowledge and application of the Word of God, as well as to become bolder in sharing God's love with those in our spheres of influence. Building up one another has been an enriching experience for each of us.

Accountability is not just for beginners. Lifelong accountability with fellow believers will reap great rewards and keep us ever on the narrow path that leads to life.

God wants you to succeed, and He will show you how to do so if you just ask Him.

> Jesus did not say anything to them [the Pharisees] without using a parable. But when He was alone with his own disciples, He explained everything. (Mark 4:34 NIV)

> He asked, "Who do you say I am?" Simon Peter answered, "You are the Messiah, the Son of the living God." Jesus replied, "Blessed are you, Simon son of Jonah, for this was not revealed to you by flesh and blood, but by My Father in heaven." (Matthew 16:15–17 NIV)

I will be accountable to:

MAROON LAKE TRAIL, MAROON BELLS, ASPEN, COLORADO

10

TRAVELING WITH PURPOSE

HAPPY GRADUATION! YOU ARE NOW TRAVELING WITH PURPOSE!

Welcome to a time of incredible affirmations! You have earned the right to hear God's truth about your position in Jesus Christ. Are you ready for some mind-blowing concepts? Sit down, get situated, and brace yourself for the gorgeous unfolding of your special place in this world.

Jesus makes it clear that we are not here on the earth to be served. Instead, we are partnering with Him to serve others and to bring glory to Father God in a variety of ways.

> For even the Son of Man did not come to be served, but to serve, and to give his life as a ransom for many. (Mark 10:45 NIV)

To serve Him properly, we need to absorb the vision that God has for you and me as His servants, which is a far cry from shabbily dressed serfs among the cinders. Much to the contrary! Instead, He sees us as His accredited envoys, representing the King of kings and the Lord of lords. Please accept these five monumental truths that propel you and me to envision how absolutely necessary we are to God's big picture via our own spheres of influence. These truths are as follows:

1. You are chosen.
2. You are called and appointed.

3. You are the aroma of Christ.
4. You are Christ's love letter to the world.
5. You are full of purpose.

In this last chapter, you will complete a worksheet for each of the five sections in lieu of homework. Are you ready to grasp your importance? Awesome, because you are truly *one selected soul* out of 8 *billion* on the planet.

TRUTH ONE: YOU ARE CHOSEN (KNOCK, KNOCK. WHO'S THERE? OR CHOSEN TO DINE WITH JESUS)

Who doesn't love a corny knock-knock joke? How about these?

Knock, knock. Who's there? Ida! Ida who? Ida rang the bell but it's out of order!

Knock, knock. Who's there? Herbert! Herbert who? Herbert flew out of its cage! There it goes!

One of my favorite verses of all time involves knocking. It's found in Revelation 3:20. Jesus says to you and me,

> "Behold, I stand at the door and knock; if anyone hears My voice and opens the door, I will come in to him and will dine with him and he with Me."

As I was dwelling on this verse with Jesus, I reflected on five ways I have answered His knock at one time or another in my life.

1. Calling through a locked door. Knock, knock. *Who's there?* Jesus! *Jesus who?* "I am Jesus whom you are persecuting" (Acts 9:5).
2. Calling through a locked door. Knock, knock. *Who's there?* Jesus! *How do You know me?* "Before I formed you in the womb I knew you. Before you were born I set you apart" (Jeremiah 1:5).
3. With the door opened a crack. Knock, knock. *Who's there?* Jesus! *Uh, it's really not a good time for a visit. I'm awfully busy today.* "I, the Lord, long to be gracious to you. I wait on high to have compassion on you" (Isaiah 30:18).
4. With the door opened for entry. Knock, knock. *Who's there?* Jesus! *Thank you for coming today. I'm sorry my house is a mess.* Jesus reached out his hand. "I am willing," he said. "Be clean!" (Matthew 8:3).
5. With the door flung open, the dinner table set with the finest china, and Christ's place at the head of the table ready and waiting for Him. Knock,

knock. *I've been expecting You. It is I, Jesus, King of kings and Lord of lords. Yes, I know You, my Savior. I'm ready to dine with You today. Please sit and stay awhile, won't You? Thank you for loving and forgiving me, regardless of my mistakes. What eye-opening insight, exceptional assignment, or selfless sacrifice do You have for me today?* "I will always satisfy you when you are weary and refresh you when you languish … I will put My law within you and on your heart I will write it. I will be your God, and you will be My child … Call to Me and I will answer you. I will tell you great and mighty things that you do not know … My grace is sufficient for you, for My power is perfected in your weakness … Tend My sheep." (Jeremiah 31:25, 33; 33:3; 2 Corinthians 12:9; John 21:17).

Our Lord and Savior never leaves the front porch but waits patiently, steadfastly, for the invitation to come in through the door of His chosen one's heart. Jesus never fails to be a gracious guest when given the opportunity to dine with us. The host or hostess gifts He brings to our tables are living water, the fruits of the Spirit, and a basketful of His bread of life. With a dinner guest like this, soon enough we will give Him the keys to our hearts so that He may make Himself at home.

Thank you, Jesus, that You have chosen to dine with me, one-on-one, at a table for two. Amen!

CHOSEN BY GOD TO BRING HIM GLORY

God holds you in high regard and will use you for His glory. He has chosen you to be a part of His glorious kingdom in heaven one day but also to promote His kingdom here on earth. A first assignment, then, is to comprehend your side of the equation by seeing your own necessity to Him.

> "I will make you like a signet ring, for I have chosen you," declares the Lord of hosts. (Haggai 2:23b NASB)

> God has chosen you from the beginning for salvation through sanctification by the Spirit and faith in the truth. It was for this He called you through our gospel, that you may gain the glory of our Lord Jesus Christ. (2 Thessalonians 2:13b–14 NASB)

Fill in the blanks for the following sentences, citing possible reasons God has chosen you as His messenger to others—your family, friends, neighbors, coworkers, and whoever you encounter from here on out.

I might fill in the blanks with these words: You love me. You need me. I am uniquely designed to_____. You have given me this talent_____.

Keep the following in mind:

> He saved us, not because of righteous things we had done, but because of his mercy. (Titus 3:5a NIV)

I am chosen by You because _____.

I am chosen by You because _____.

I am chosen by You because _____.

I am chosen by You because _____.

I am chosen by You because _____.

I am chosen by You because _____.

I am chosen by You because _____.

I am chosen by You because _____.

I am chosen by You because _____.

I am chosen by You because _____.

Dear Jesus, forgive me for not seeing myself as You see me, a child of the King of kings. I am honored and ready for service. Amen.

TRUTH TWO: YOU ARE CALLED AND APPOINTED (WHAT IS YOUR CALL?)

One of the most life-changing concepts we can appropriate is to know without a doubt that we are called by God for a purpose on this earth. In fact, throughout our lives, our calls can change from one role to another. Jeremiah 1:4–5 (NIV) is an important verse in this understanding:

The Call of Jeremiah

The word of the Lord came to me, saying, "Before I formed you in the womb I knew you, before you were born, I set you apart; I appointed you as a prophet to the nations."

Now, let's take this verse and make it our own:

"[Your name here], before I formed you in the womb I knew you, before you were born, I set you apart; I appointed you as a_____ to your _____."

As you review your life, what are some of the "calls" God has given to you?

- After my firstborn daughter, Ricki, went off to kindergarten, I heard God say, *"Cindy, I appoint you as a homeschool teacher to your children."* The next year, I obediently began to homeschool Ricki in first grade and my second-born, Amy, in kindergarten. Throughout the years, my younger four children—Kelly, Susie, Tom, and Jack—took their own places at the dining room table for all or some portion of their schooling too.
- When my sweet mother needed daily assistance, I heard God say, *"Cindy, I appoint you as a caregiver to your mother."* She came to live with my family for the last four years of her life.
- When I wondered what was next for me after my mom's heaven-bound passing, I heard God say, *"Cindy, I appoint you as a hospice caregiver to the dying."*

These are just a few examples of the many calls the Lord has had on my life. Take time to reflect, and you, too, will have undoubtedly served God through a variety of calls on your own life.

What is your call right now? How is God using you at this moment to make a difference for Him? Perhaps it is as a prayer warrior, a confidant, a mentor, a spokesperson, a peacemaker, an encourager, a servant, a leader, a stable supporter. You likely have several different calls going on at the same time.

It is good to take stock of how God is using us. Let us put a name to these calls so we will know for what purposes we are set apart as His ministers. Whatever we are, we are always allies to our living God.

YOUR MANY APPOINTMENTS

You are uniquely stamped, approved by the Creator Himself, and appointed for certain assignments. These appointments are known to you and are a part of your everyday life, such as child, spouse, parent, relative, friend, student, employer, coworker, employee, trainee, coach, teacher, nurse, specialist, mechanic, builder, gardener, cook, driver, banker. List the multitude of appointments you have been given, and gain a new perspective on your godly influence over those to whom you have been assigned.

"Before I formed you in the womb I knew you, and before you were born, I consecrated you; I have appointed you, _____, to be a _____, to your_____" (Jeremiah 1:5 NIV).

I am a _____to my _____.
I am a _____to my _____.
I am a _____to my _____.
I am a _____to my _____.
I am a _____to my _____.
I am a _____to my _____.
I am a _____to my _____.
I am a _____to my _____.
I am a _____to my _____.
I am a _____to my _____.

Dear Jesus, I have been appointed by You to be a light to my world. I am important to You and to my sphere of influence. Thank you for this remarkable and divine calling. Let me remember daily Your need for my godly influence in the lives of these people. Amen.

TRUTH THREE: YOU ARE THE AROMA OF CHRIST (AROMA-OF-CHRIST THERAPY)

In my life, I remember two very distinct aromatherapies I received. The most pleasant one was when I traveled to Hawaii with my husband, Leo. I remember stepping off the plane and being struck with a beautiful, soothing aroma of fragrant flowers. This pleasing perfume wafted throughout the island of Maui wherever we went. It was the enchanting bouquet of plumeria. I wondered if the people of the island were affected by it daily too or if it had become an accustomed scent to them.

My second striking aromatherapy happened when I was a child and drove with my parents to the town of Greeley, Colorado. Along the rural route, the strong odor of sugar beets, mingled with the smell of the stockyards, carved its way into my mind forever. When Leo and I moved to Greeley during our first year of marriage for his new employment and my last year of college, I wondered if we, too, would smell the stench daily or would get used to it. Hmmm. (Good news! The wind blows in favor of the residents.)

Paul penned that you and I give off an aroma that God loves, the aroma of His Son, Jesus.

> But thanks be to God, who always leads us as captives in Christ's triumphal procession and uses us to spread the aroma of the knowledge of him everywhere. For we are to God the pleasing aroma of Christ among those who are being saved and those who are perishing. (2 Corinthians 2:14–15 NIV)

As you and I are honored to be Christ's representatives, it gives us pause to examine the odor we emit. Is it delightful, fragrant plumeria, representative of the beautiful person Christ works to transform within your soul and mine? Or do we still reek of the stockyards from the old life and its practices? The goal is to bring a welcome, attractive aroma-of-Christ therapy to the world around us, wherever we travel. Let's bathe daily in His Word and ways and thus carry His heavenly scent with us along the path of life.

EVEN FRAGRANT IN SETBACKS

You and I are the "knowledge of Christ," and people around us sense (or "scents") this. Take stock of the unpleasant situations you are now facing. What aromatic responses might be emitted, and who would be affected by such a pleasing perfume? The goal is to be fragrant, even in smelly circumstances.

My Unpleasant Situation	My Fragrant Response
_____	_____
_____	_____
_____	_____
_____	_____
_____	_____

Dear Jesus, I take You with me wherever I go, as You reside within me. I will always encounter many difficult situations. Give me aroma-of-Christ responses to them. Let me be honored to emit a pleasing aroma, even while ascending the steep hills of life. Amen.

TRUTH FOUR: YOU ARE CHRIST'S LOVE LETTER TO THE WORLD (A LIVING, BREATHING CHRISTMAS LETTER)

What are your thoughts about Christmas letters? While I love receiving them from dear friends, there was a time in my life when I took a long break from writing them because my life was anything but exciting. It was hard. Real hard. And hard lives don't make for happy Christmas news.

As I pondered this thought, the Lord brought my fingers to rest on Paul's second, encouraging letter to the believers at Corinth:

> You yourselves are our letter, written on our hearts, known and read by everyone. You show that you are a letter from Christ, the result of our ministry, written not with ink but with the Spirit of the living God, not on tablets of stone but on tablets of human hearts. (2 Corinthians 3:2–3 NIV)

I realized that my own life, in and of itself, if lived for Jesus Christ, is a Christmas letter to those in my sphere of influence. Even if I never sent out another Christmas letter, I can rest assured that I am Christ's Christmas letter, opened and read by others, and you are too! He has sent us, sealed and stamped with forever postage, to the people at work, in our neighborhoods, and at the shopping center.

These letters of our lives are not written on festive card stock but instead are written heart by heart, kind word by kind word, loving action by loving action, hard assignment by hard assignment. Ours is a Christmas message sent out moment by moment, all year long. The message is this: Jesus, also known as the Word, came from heaven, became flesh, and dwelled among us to reconcile us to God.

> In the beginning was the Word, and the Word was with God, and the Word was God. He was with God in the beginning. Through him all things were made; without him nothing was made that has been made. In him was life, and that life was the light of all mankind. The light shines in the darkness, and the darkness has not overcome it … The Word became flesh and made his dwelling among us. We have seen his glory, the glory of the one and only Son, who came from the Father, full of grace and truth. (John 1:1–4, 14 NIV)

YOUR PERSONAL MISSION FIELD

Wherever you go, people will see who Jesus is through you. You are Christ's love letter, written on His heart and sent out to everyone you encounter. List the names of persons known to you to whom the Lord has sent you as His special-delivery communiqué.

I am a letter of Christ, sent to_____.
I am a letter of Christ, sent to_____.
I am a letter of Christ, sent to_____.
I am a letter of Christ, sent to_____.
I am a letter of Christ, sent to_____.
I am a letter of Christ, sent to_____.
I am a letter of Christ, sent to_____.
I am a letter of Christ, sent to_____.

Dear Jesus, I am Your letter to people, showing them who You are. Help me to display love, kindness, mercy, and enormous faith to all who see Your image in me. Amen.

Truth Five: You Are Full of Purpose (You: Designed by God for a Great Purpose)

It is difficult to escape the message of the media that we don't measure up. We are not tall enough, thin enough, athletic enough, famous enough, cool enough, fashion-savvy enough, rich enough, smart enough, and "enough" enough. It is easy to follow after false dreams and bubbles that burst when we rely on the entertainment industry to define our significance.

God has designed each one of us as a person of worth and value, with gifts and talents to share with the world. God chose a man named Bezalel to bring beauty to the wilderness by using his talents in helping to craft God's desert dwelling place, the Tabernacle.

> Then Moses said to the sons of Israel, "See, the Lord has called by name Bezalel … And He has filled him with the Spirit of God, in wisdom, in understanding and in knowledge and in all craftsmanship; to make designs for working in gold and in silver and in bronze, and in the cutting of stones for settings and in the carving of wood, so as to perform in every inventive work. (Exodus 35:30–33 NIV)

Like Bezalel, you are a chosen vessel, handpicked by God with unique qualities and skills to affect your sphere of influence for His glory. Consider yourself distinctive, exceptional, necessary, needed, phenomenal, remarkable, unrivaled, and valuable just as you are—designed by the master craftsman Himself for great purposes!

Dear Jesus, I am full of purpose. Let me always believe that. Use me to be a life, family, and sphere-of-influence changer. May You go before me every step of the journey that we travel together. Amen.

Possible Purposes

The Lord knows your future assignments and has work for you to do. Yet He would also like to hear about your secret yearnings of service.

What are your heart's desires in serving Jesus? List ways you might like to be used by Him. Pray about it, and prepare to hear back from Him regarding your dreams.

> May the Lord grant you your heart's desire and fulfill all your purposes!
> (Psalm 20:4 NASB)

I desire to be a _____ to _____.

I desire to be a _____ to _____.

I desire to be a _____ to _____.

I desire to be a _____ to _____.

I desire to be a _____ to _____.

I desire to be a _____ to _____.

I desire to be a _____ to _____.

I desire to be a _____ to _____.

Dear Jesus, You have purposes for me that I could never even imagine. Help me be ready to fulfill these purposes by staying ever so close to You in our intimate times together. May I listen as You instruct me in the way I should go. Here's to us, together, for Your glory! Amen.

YOUR JESUS JOURNEY: MISSION ACCOMPLISHED!

You have traveled well this final leg of the journey. You now know that God has put His stamp of approval upon you, commissioned you for great service, and is delighted that you will partner with Him in being used and sent out to your own personal sphere of influence.

Please continue to employ Daily Retreat, using scripture reflection as a means of hearing from Jesus, discerning His assignments for your day, and receiving His orders to accomplish your purposes here on earth. Life becomes extremely far-reaching from this beautiful scenic overlook.

SINNER/SAVED/SENT! ALL WE NEED TO KNOW FOR THE JOURNEY AHEAD

So, my friend, what has been consequential to your life these past weeks? What did you find most encouraging? How have you grown and changed since you first opened this book?

As you and I follow Jesus's charted course for us for the rest of our lives, let us cleave to the simple truth that we are forgiven sinners, saved by the grace of God through His only Son, Jesus Christ, and sent out by God to share His love with others. Sinner/Saved/Sent! That's it!

As we wrap our minds around the new mindset that we are "non-secret" agents of Jesus Christ, living in victory, and sharing His good news, it makes ordinary life exciting and momentous. As we slide into our automobiles from the scenic overlook, merge back onto the highway of life, and forge forward in faith, may the power of Jesus Christ propel us to His purposed destinations.

I look forward to meeting you along life's way. I will know you because I will see my sweet Lord and Savior Jesus in you. Thank you for reflecting Him so handsomely, so beautifully!

> And a great road will go through that once deserted land. It will be named the Highway of Holiness. Evil-minded people will never travel on it. It will be only for those who walk in God's ways. (Isaiah 35:8 NLT)

Dear Jesus, please take our new friend safely along this earthly highway of holiness. May this dear beloved of Yours relate one-on-one with You regularly, and may You, dear Jesus, be ever faithful and true to Your number one-in-eight-billion intimate. In Your name, I pray for this particular, exceptional person. Amen.

GOD'S BLESSING TO YOU

May the Lord bless you and protect you.
May the Lord smile on you and be gracious to you.
May the Lord show you his favor and give you his peace.

—Numbers 6:24–26 (NLT)

Acknowledgments

Thank you, Father God, for creating me. Thank you, Lord Jesus, for saving me. Thank you, Holy Spirit, for empowering me. I owe everything to You, my one, true God-in-Three Persons, blessed Trinity.

In loving memory of my parents, Dale and Theda Adams; my mother-in-law, Marianne Oury; my father-in-law, John Oury, and his second wife, Jeanne Radysh Oury—all believers who are now enjoying resurrected life in Christ. Thank you, Dad O., for your investment in this book!

In awe of my faithful husband, Leo Oury, who led me to the Lord, forgives me for my wrongs, and stands beside me in every joy and hardship of life. Thank you for your unending support, plus your selflessly obedient role in bringing *Your Jesus Journey* to others.

A thankful heart for my beautiful, unique six children and their families: Ricki and Kevin, Felicity and Jace; Amy and John; Kelly and Dwayne and Elam; Susie and Garret, Waylon and Wren; Tom and Jayne; Jack and Leigh and Baby-to-be. You've helped me travel my Jesus journey, right by my side.

In appreciation for my sisters: Susie Phillips, benevolent and encouraging throughout my life, plus Jessica and Jeremy, Sollie and Ethan, and Jake; Kay Adams, counselor, author, founder of the Center for Journal Therapy and *Your Jesus Journey* early editor and her husband, Ken Perreault.

Beloved relatives: Leo's siblings Tom and Pam, Sue and Jeff, Peter and Tavia, Liz and Norb and their families, and Leo's extended family including Aunt Alice, David and Debby, Cousin Sarah and their families; my Oregon Cousins Cotty and Tom, Kevin and Anne, Janet, John and their families.

Ageless friendships: Lisa (and Jim), Cathy (and Ned), Carol (and Bob)—my school-years besties in Arvada; Claire and Jim, Julie and John, Laura—my college-years besties in Wisconsin; Greg and Sherry, Mark (now in heaven) and Casey in Greeley; Barb, who taught me quiet time; lifelong mentors Terry and Suzi, plus Curt and Lucy, Dan and Molly in Colorado Springs; Arvada friends: Sharon—warrior who advances the gospel; Debbie (and Jim L.)—who took me on the Bible-in-a-year excursion, along with Tammy (and John), Elizabeth (and Todd), Darlene (and Rich), Irene (and Steve) who got together with me to study the Word of God at 5:30 a.m. back in the day; Gary and Amy, Brian and Amy, Tim and Holly, Lon and Nerene, Dave and Kathleen, Jason and Lucille, John and Jodi, Scott and Laurie, Scott and Lisa, plus others mentioned already who did small group together in our 30's and 40's; John and Dottie, Bruce and Sara, Steve and Terri, Alan and Emily, Tania, Dan and Earen, Mike and Darlene, Dave and Renae, Jim and Debbie B.; Santiago and Cindy, George and Leah, Betty and more Colorado ACTS friends.

Women's Group Attendees, 2009 to 2014: Patty, Sharon H., Sharon M., Susan, Lynn, Tania, Tosha, Pat, Paula, Linda, Leslie, Laurie, Karen, Dara, Denise, Chris, Katie, Gaylene, Jodi, Jen, Nancy, and Linda J., now in heaven.

Bible Scholars Class, 2015 to present: Jim and Sonci, Kevin and Lynn, Kirk and Linda, Neil and Dara, Leo, Lisa, Deb, Tim and Karen, Margaret, Diana, Linda, Kristi, Andy, Kathy, Janice, Creg and Terri, Art and Vicki, and Ruby, now in heaven.

January/February 2023 Your Jesus Journey Pilot Class: Denise, Parker, Alex, Grant, George, Shirley B., Liz, Steve, Shirley M., Cheryl, Elizabeth, Gary, Heather, Joy, Hannah, Ed, Julie, LeJeane, and Donni.

October/November 2023 Your Jesus Journey Pre-Publication Class: Robin, Roger, Jean, Miriya, Evie, Michele, Joanne, Keith, Bill, Leo, Gloria, Reyna, Marty, and Jeanette.

4C's Family of Believers: You are my people.

4C's Staff: Pastors Brian, Dave, Nathan, Scott, Gloria, Clarene, plus Donni, Joanne, Brittany, Elise, Claire, Brian, Jim, and Tim.

Last but, according to Jesus, sacrificially first:

Publisher: WestBow Press and my specific team members: Eric, Georgette, Denise, John, Marna, Janine, Faye, and the design team.

Photographer: Valerie Mills, VP Photography

Providers: Jesus, John, and Leo in tandem

Early Editor: Kathleen Adams

Special Book Assistance: Patty, Lisa, and Donni

Precious, Longtime Prayer Partners: Gloria, Marty, and Robin

All without whom this book would not be in your hands.

To God be the glory,

Amen.

Printed in the United States
by Baker & Taylor Publisher Services